Follow Your Heart

The True Story of Terry Wilks

by

Joan Dew
and
David Fox

Pacific Press Publishing Association
Boise, Idaho
Oshawa, Ontario, Canada

JOAN DEW and DAVID FOX reside in Nashville, Tennessee. Ms. Dew has written many books including autobiographies of Tammy Wynette and Minnie Pearl. Mr. Fox was a journalist for 12 years. He has written three other books and currently works for a public relations agency in Nashville.

Terry and Gilbert Wilks assume full responsibility for the accuracy of the camera-ready copy of this book. Editing, copyediting and proofreading for this book were under the direction of Wilks Publications.

Designed by Tim Larson
Cover by Bill Myers

Library of Congress Catalog Card Number: 87-62719

ISBN 0-8163-0761-X

PROLOGUE

How could we have known that on February 19, 1981, at 5:23 p.m. the life of our family would be changed forever. A half-second misjudgement of time on a double-forward flip, and Terry, our 18-year-old son, lay paralyzed on the gymnasium floor.

"Why can't he get up? This is temporary. Once he gets to the hospital, he'll be okay." We were so sure.

But as the weeks and months went by we slowly began to realize that Terry, the "special guy" who ran, jumped, rode horses, and drove our family car would probably never do those things again.

We had to accept the reality that what had happened to our son had happened to our FAMILY. We also have come to realize that this is unquestionably true for every family when tragedy strikes one of its members. We saw it in the eyes and heard it in the voices of so many other families during those long months we spent in hospitals.

How would we get through it? Would our lives ever be happy and exciting again? Would our close family be damaged in some way that could leave us permanently scarred? Was this to be a test of our faith in God? And if so, would we pass it?

"Oh God!" we prayed, "if You will just allow Terry to walk. Or just give him the use of his hands!"

But the answer to our prayers did not come in the movement of Terry's body. Instead it came in his attitude.

This is the story of our family's struggle to conquer disaster, to accept the unacceptable and to make the best of it.

We have shared our personal lives with you not because we want to share a tragedy, but because we want to share hope, comfort, inspiration and joy. It is our prayer that on these pages you will find some of each.

THE WILKS FAMILY

MY THANKS TO...

My Family --they're wonderful
       and I love them.

My Friends --thru the good and the bad;
       you've always made my life better.

My God   --He's a real part of me.

Patty Christman --for the 100's of hours she spent
       collecting the facts for my story;
       and most of all, her love and
       understanding.

Dr. Barth Green --for his extra efforts to cure
       paralysis.

CONTENTS

INTRODUCTION

ACCIDENTS HAPPEN.

In homes across the United States every day, families are having their lives changed irrevocably by unexpected injury. There are 36 million disabled Americans, 16% of the population. If you add family members to this, fully a third of the U.S. population is affected by disabilities.

The loss is significant in many ways.

It is a drain on our national resources; $1^{00} out of every $12^{00} spent by the federal government is for direct payments to disabled Americans, or to fund programs for them.

National productivity is hurt as well, since unemployment among disabled Americans is 62%.

But the true price of an accident cannot be found in national statistics. It is in the lives of the people affected. This is the story of a family, "normal" by most standards, who has lived through the tragedy of an accident, yet persevered to witness the triumph of the human spirit, as the accident's "victim" won the battle -- first to survive, and then to gain control of his own life.

Getting to know Terry Wilks during the course of writing this book was both enlightening and inspiring. Neither of us had ever been around a quadriplegic. What would it be like, spending hours, days and weeks with someone who was paralyzed from the neck down? Whatever else, we didn't anticipate it being a lot of fun. We were wrong.

Of course there were sad times -- times when we cried, times when we felt overwhelmed, DEVASTATED by Terry's condition and his altered life. But what we remember most vividly about the times spent with Terry is laughter, warmth and that mischievous glint in his eye when he was about to tell us some outrageous idea he'd just had. And always, on our way home after being with Terry, we felt inspired by his indomitable spirit.

We learned that to see life through Terry Wilks' eyes is to see that the human being and the body it inhabits are two entirely different things. Even for the most athletic and developed physical specimens on this earth, the body is only a vehicle. The human being inhabits that body, the way a driver inhabits a car. Even though Terry has the use of only a fraction of his body, the human being inside is still whole and intact.

While working on the book we read a newspaper artical about actor John Ritter's brother Tom, who has cerebral palsy. He was quoted as saying: "My mother's music was lyrical music to the soul, keeping out the QUIET PAIN OF BEING DIFFERENT." Reading it we thought, 'That's Terry! That's what makes Terry so special. He has learned how to deal with the QUIET PAIN by creating his own 'lyrical music to the soul'.'

What we learned from Terry is a universal message: If we could see others as separate in Body and in Being, we would be able to communicate on a new level. We wouldn't judge others by the shape of their nose, the color of their skin or the extent of their disability, but as Martin Luther King said, we would judge them by the CONTENT OF THEIR CHARACTER. In order to see others this way, however, we must first learn to separate our own Body from our Being. That is what Terry Wilks has done. This book shares the experiences, the will and the faith that enabled him to do that.

Joan Dew
David Fox
Nashville, Tennessee
1987

"Terry,
Stand Up!"

FEBRUARY 19, 1981

5:30 a.m.—The buzzing sound came to him through a thick haze of sleep, growing louder until finally he recognized it— the alarm clock. With an effort he shut it off. It was pitch black outside and cold from the lingering February night. The impulse to fall back to sleep lasted only a second before Terry pushed himself up and stumbled down the hall to the bathroom on legs still sore from the previous day's practice.

As he began brushing his teeth, his mind wandered to a dream he vaguely remembered. He had been riding a horse and a girl had been on the horse with him. It was Joanne, his old girlfriend, but later in the dream, it had become Jonetta. Terry looked in the mirror and shook his head. "Women," he said.

Back in bed, Terry leaned against the wall of barnwood, picking up his Bible and glancing across the room at the four drawings of horses on the opposite wall. He had painted them himself when he was in the seventh grade and won four blue ribbons at a local art show. They'd been on the wall for five years now, and it seemed like three years since he'd even noticed them. One of these days he was going to get back to his drawing.

He opened the Bible to the book of John, Chapter 12, and began reading, "Now is my soul troubled, and what shall I say? 'Father save me from this hour.' "

His eyes continued to move over the words, but his thoughts returned to Jonetta. He could see her laughing now, as he dangled her shoe in front of her. They were in study hall just the day before and she'd had her foot propped up on the desk beside his.

"What'll you give me?" Terry asked suggestively and Jonetta smiled her flirtatious smile. "Just give me my shoe back, or else. . . ."

"Or else what?"

"Or else I'll never go out with you."

He smiled mischievously. "Does that mean if I give it to you, you WILL go out with me?"

"Maybe."

He stuck the shoe in his notebook. "I want a firm answer."

"Terry!"

He begrudgingly handed her the shoe. "You sure are a hard person to bargain with," he said, and she smiled that sweet smile at him again.

What was it about her? Why the distance? He'd never get to know her if she wouldn't even go out with him.

"Great," Terry said to himself as the Bible in his lap came back into focus. He'd almost finished the chapter and hadn't paid attention to a word he'd read. He went back to the beginning and started over. This time, he knew, he wouldn't miss a word.

* * *

7 a.m.—"Terry, you're going to be late!"

He bounded up the stairs and hustled into the kitchen for breakfast. "Diane's already finished," his mother said, as he sat down to his first bowl of oatmeal.

"Don't worry, Mom, everything's under control."

Myrna watched her son wolf down the oatmeal with a mother's concern for his digestion. Terry never left the table before he'd devoured two or three helpings of everything. Despite his ravenous eating habits and muscular physique, however, Terry was still the lightest member of the gymnastics team.

"If you want any clothes washed, bring them upstairs before you leave," she said, and Terry nodded at her with his mouth full as Diane came into the kitchen, ready to leave for school.

"We're going to be late," she said to Terry and he did his best to ignore her. "It's seven-FIFTEEN."

"All right, all right."

Myrna stood at the top of the steps as Terry stopped to hand her a basket of dirty clothes.

"Thanks for breakfast, Mom. See you this afternoon."

He smiled at her and as he turned and trotted out to the car, she was struck by her son's physique. His shoulders were becoming so broad and his hips were still narrow. There was a spring in his step. She smiled to herself as she went back to wake up little David, thinking about what a fine young man her oldest son was turning out to be.

* * *

Diane was in the tenth grade and just old enough to start driving; so Terry had agreed to let her drive them to the campus where they would spend the morning working and the afternoon attending classes. That was the routine for half the students at Highland Academy. The other half went to school in the morning and worked in the afternoon. It was a schedule common among Seventh-day Adventist schools, where learning a trade and classroom education were considered equally important to the educational process.

As they drove onto the Highland Academy campus, Terry looked around at the environment that had been his home for almost ten years and wondered exactly what he was supposed to feel, now that he was about to graduate. Was he happy or sad? Was he going to miss this place? He didn't know, and now was not the time to think about it anyway. If God wanted him to feel something, he'd feel it. Otherwise, he had plenty to keep his mind occupied without a lot of daydreaming. Especially since they had already arrived at work.

Terry got out of the car and headed for the side entrance to Wilks Publications, where he and Diane would spend their morning working alongside fifteen other students from the academy. As he crossed the gravel parking lot, he glanced at the window on the far left hand side of the building—his father's office. Someday it would be his office. If he was good enough.

* * *

10 a.m.—"Clackety, clackety, clackety."

The press churned out page after page with a tireless, endless consistency. The sound of it had become an indelible part of Terry's memory, like the sound of crickets outside his bedroom at night, or the harmonies of the Highland Church Choir.

He'd worked around this press for years and could still remember "the good old days" when he'd fall asleep in a corner of the press room while his mother and father worked late. Now, the sound came to him during the day, when he'd catch himself daydreaming. "Clackety-clack," he'd say to himself and his thoughts would turn back to the task at hand. Terry wanted to teach himself to be more like the press. Productive, dependable, indistractible.

He picked up another stack of pages and carried them into the sorting room, then returned to check the ink level.

As he walked past the camera room on his way back to the press, Terry resisted the urge to stop and watch his classmates working with the layouts for next week's publication. The only reason he wasn't working in the camera room himself was because the production manager thought he worked too slowly. He went to too much trouble with simple tasks, laboring over details that would never be noticed. There just wasn't enough time for that much perfection.

* * *

12:30 p.m.—Lunchtime. The cafeteria was crowded as Terry got in line. He was starving as usual, and loaded his plate with enough food for three people. When the girl ahead of him dropped her fork, Terry picked it up and got her a clean one.

He found a seat at a table with Rosalie and Lori, and did his best to join in the conversation as he wolfed down his lunch. They were talking about marriage. Lori was depressed because Randy wasn't ready to set a date for their wedding. Terry tried to comfort her, thinking about his own break-up with Joanne.

Joanne and he had looked forward to their life together as man and wife almost from the day they began dating, two years before. Then, suddenly, she'd turned cold toward him. She didn't want to talk about their future together, as they once had, and he couldn't understand it. Was he doing something wrong? How could she no longer love him, when he still loved her so much?

He had done everything he could think of to win her back, but the more he tried, the more distant she became. The pain of that rejection had etched a deep lesson in his consciousness.Girls were trouble. They sapped all your strength. Better to concentrate on business. Think about your net worth. Now that was something Terry had always enjoyed thinking about, ever since his mother helped him open his first savings account when he was four years old. Terry was 18 now and was worth more than a thousand dollars. He had enough money to buy his own horse and his own car. Maybe a 1970 blue Dodge wasn't the hottest thing on the road, but it was his. Besides, a car couldn't break your heart. No, there definitely was no reason for him to be worrying about girls now. There was too much work to be done. Clackety-clack.

* * *

1 p.m.—History was his first class after lunch, and somehow he managed to fight off the temptation to fall asleep. Temptations, Terry believed, were his biggest enemy.

There was a story that made the rounds about Terry after he'd taken the college entrance exam his senior year. The test was administered in the science classroom, and the last two questions of the test dealt with chemical elements. On the wall at the front of the class was the periodic chart of elements. One look at the chart and Terry could have answered the questions, but he didn't know if it was allowed, so he kept his head down and answered the questions without looking.

His friends started calling Terry 'Honest Abe' after he told them about it and that made him feel stupid and naive. But at the same time, there had been a real and private sense of satisfaction when he walked out of that classroom, knowing he'd overcome temptation one more time.

* * *

4 p.m.—Classes were over. Terry was standing in front of his locker, when Robbie Elliott walked up. Robbie was a junior and Terry's best friend at Highland.

"I hear you get to make the big speech at graduation," said Robbie.

Terry shrugged. "At the baccalaureate service. I have to answer the challenge for the senior class."

Robbie nodded. "Know what you're going to say?"

"That's three months away," Terry said, arranging his books in the locker and taking a piece of paper out of his notebook.

"We're going to be late for practice," Robbie said.

"Look at this." Terry handed the paper to Robbie as they started walking. It was the design for a hovercraft, which he had received in the mail after responding to an ad in the back of *Popular Mechanics Magazine*.

"So this is what you're going to build?"

"Yeah, but I think I'll need a bigger prop."

Robbie handed it back to Terry. "Forget it, Wilks," he said. "It'll never fly."

As they walked out into the cool afternoon mist and started down the hill toward the gym, Terry's mind was on graduation again. He thought about the speech he would make, as pastor of his graduating class. It would be a moment of triumph for him. He pictured himself stepping forward to receive his diploma, hearing Mr. Brewer's voice in his mind:

"Pastor of the student association and pastor of his class for two years. Best all-around gymnast. Member of the annual staff. Member of band and choir. And voted by the senior class, Most Courteous and Most Likely to Succeed."

Most likely to succeed. The words had played in his head since the day he'd won the honor. It was not like all the other awards—not like most talented or most athletic, which honored past success. Most likely to succeed was a prediction of future success, and that was an expectation Terry intended to live up to.

"Come on," he said to Robbie, breaking into a jog. "We're going to be late for practice."

* * *

4:30 p.m.—The rest of the team was already warming up as Terry emerged from the locker room in his gym shorts and favorite green T-shirt and started his five warmup laps around the gym. Life usually started coming back into his legs after the third lap.

On his fourth lap he saw Coach emerge from the locker room and he angled across the gym to join the others.

"Okay, guys," Coach was saying. "Tomorrow we leave for Louisville and we want to look sharp. Let's work hard today. Everybody concentrate on your individual routines for 30 minutes and then we'll work on mat passes."

The boys nodded and gathered in close around Coach for the prayer that started every practice. Then he clapped his hands and practice began.

Terry rubbed the chalk brick over the thick callouses he'd developed in three years of gymnastics. His first exercise would be the parallel bars, since that was the routine he would perform at the Louisville exhibition the next day.

He placed his arms on the bars, swung his legs forward and lifted himself into action. The mount was tricky, but after a couple of false starts, he got it right and moved into his routine, swinging gracefully between the bars, rising to a full handstand, swinging forward then up again, gripping the bars firmly as he moved toward the final handstand and his spinning dismount.

He caked his hands while Mark followed him on the bars, until it was his turn again. Repetition. That was the secret. Practice and practice until there were no more mistakes.

As he swung up to begin his second routine, he looked down at the mat and remembered his worst fall as a gymnast. He'd been working on the parallel bars. His feet hadn't come over far enough on a dive dismount and he'd landed on his head, straight down. The pain had lasted for days, but he'd kept practicing. That was the thing about gymnastics, you took a lot of falls and you just had to keep getting back up and moving on to the next routine.

* * *

4:55 p.m.—After 25 minutes, Terry had had enough of the parallel bars. "Let's do some vaulting," he yelled at Pat and Sam nearby.

"Sure," Pat said and they pulled the springboard, mats and vault box out to the center of the gym floor. Terry loved vaulting. It was the most exciting of the gymnastic events, because when he hit the springboard after a good running start, he felt like a jet taking off.

The vault box was there for the added lift from the handspring, but after a few vaults, Terry suggested they try some flips without the box.

He and Pat pushed it out of the way. By this time, most of the other team members had moved on to other routines. Coach was spotting the girls' pyramid routine. It was just Terry and Pat, two of the best gymnasts on the team, working on the springboard.

When Terry watched Pat work out, he knew the other boy was a better gymnast. His forms and technique were better, but Terry had been voted best all-around gymnast, because he worked hard to achieve more.

After a series of front flips off the springboard, Terry was feeling good. When he was feeling good, the jumps seemed so effortless.

"Let's try a double," he said to Pat, who shrugged and agreed. Terry stepped to the starting line. He'd been talking about doing a double front flip for weeks. He'd never even tried one. Now's as good a time as any, he said to himself, staring down the runway at the springboard and focusing all his concentration on that small wedge of wood.

"Arms loose. Long strides. Speed is crucial. Hips and legs forward when I hit the board. Body rigid. Spike into the prime of the board. Height. At the top of the jump, concave chest, arms and upper body swing down. Knees to chest. Tight ball, the tighter the better. Flip once. Stay tucked. Flip twice. DON'T UNRAVEL TOO SOON."

Eyes riveted on the springboard, Terry took off. He hit the springboard at full speed and soared toward the dark gray rafters above. Flip once, tight, flip. . . . No. He came out of the tuck just a fraction out of instinct. Another flip but it was too late. He'd lost the momentum. . . .

He landed with a thud on his shoulders, and sprawled forward. For a second he lay still, making sure he was all right, then rolled over and pushed himself up.

"Came out of my tuck too soon," he said to Pat as he walked back to the starting line, flexing his shoulders. It hurt some, but he'd had worse falls.

"Gonna try it again?" Pat asked.

"Yeah, I just need to hold my tuck. I think I can do it."

Fred Curry sat in the bleachers, watching Terry prepare for his second attempt at the double front flip. Fred was an anesthetist at the Highland Medical Center, and a good friend of the Wilks family. His wife, Nancy, was sitting beside him. They had come to watch their daughter, Candy, who had recently joined the girls gymnastics team.

"Look how far back Terry gets to start his run," Nancy remarked.

"Yeah, he always gives it a hundred and ten percent," Fred replied, noticing the determination in Terry's eyes as he started down the runway. He was moving fast but still under control when he hit the springboard and soared into his first flip.'He's not spinning fast enough,' Fred thought. As Terry came around for the second flip, his tuck had loosened again. His knees were away from his chest and his head was back. He'd barely started the second flip when his forehead hit the mat. His body continued to flip over and as it did, his head was forced all the way back, until the momentum finally carried him over. Nancy Curry jumped from her seat with a gasp and Fred stared at the body, sprawled on the gym floor. "Come on, Terry," he said, standing up now himself. "Move."

* * *

Terry tried to orient himself to the pain. This time it was different. He had heard a pop. What was it? He felt paralyzed. He needed to get out of the way so Pat could go. 'If I don't move and he doesn't see me, he'll land right on me,' Terry thought. But nothing happened.

"What's wrong?" It was Sam, leaning over him. Terry managed a smile. "Get Coach," he said. His mind was racing. Everything was different. His legs felt cramped, constricted, as if he'd been zipped into a skin tight sleeping bag. His head was caught at a weird angle and he had to concentrate to breathe. If he could just move his legs.

"What's wrong, Ter?"

It was Coach, and behind him, Fred Curry.

"You okay, Terry?" Fred asked.

"I think I broke my neck," Terry said, and the two men stared at him, speechless. "Please move my legs."

"Don't touch him!" Coach almost shouted, as Robbie started toward Terry. "Let's try to get his head off that mat, but move him as little as possible."

Terry grimaced as his head was moved out of a crack between two mats. If they would just move his legs, so he'd know they were still there. He couldn't even feel them.

Their words were coming to him through a strange, buzzing shield of pain. He opened his eyes and saw Robbie.

"Call my Dad," he said. "But tell him I'm all right."

As Robbie ran to the phone, Terry closed his eyes again. He

knew he wasn't all right. Then his thoughts were replaced by a new wave of pain that seemed to swell up from his body and roll into his head like an electrical storm, crashing and thrashing. It was all he could do to fight it off. He'd fallen playing tennis once and hit his head on the concrete court. This pain was like that, except that it kept coming. If they'd just move his legs so he could get comfortable. . . .

People began to float in front of him. There were two medics from the hospital in white, kneeling over him. "Can you feel this?" one of them said, but there was no feeling.

"What about here?"

Then he saw his father leaning over him. He tried to smile, to reassure his Dad that everything was okay, but he knew it wasn't. He'd really pulled a big one this time.

"Okay, Terry, we're going to put you on a stretcher, and take you over to the hospital."

The medic moved the stretcher beside Terry. "Hold on now."

As they reached under him to turn him, such an intense wave of pain shot through him that he had to struggle to stay conscious. Things were becoming dark. He was becoming delirious. The stretcher was half way under him and they were pushing the other half up when the second wave hit. More intense than the first. All he could do was make himself keep breathing and try to hold himself together until the pain left, but the pain wouldn't leave.

When he opened his eyes again, exhausted, he was being carried out of the gym through a crowd of his friends and classmates. He could see some of them were crying and his heart went out to them. If only they knew how much he appreciated their friendship.

Lori and Gerald were standing at the door. As Terry was carried past them, he managed a faint smile. Lori leaned over, the tears streaming down her face. "Just remember," he said, "I love you all."

Fighting Hard

Myrna was in the last stages of fixing dinner when Gilbert called from the gym. His voice was calm, but she could detect a note of concern. "Terry's been hurt," Gilbert said. "I don't think it's serious but I think you ought to come down here."

In five minutes she had dinner on hold and David bundled up for the trip to his grandmother's house. "Don't worry unless you know what you're worried about." She repeated the words silently to herself as she hurried to the car.

There was a crowd outside the medical center's emergency entrance when Myrna pulled into the parking lot. "He's going to be okay," someone said as she got out of the car and made her way inside. First she saw Gilbert, then Terry. He was on a stretcher with two sandbags on either side of his head that made her gasp.

Terry struggled to smile at her when she reached his side. "Hey, Mom," he whispered.

"Just relax, honey," she said, wanting to cry, "I'm right here."

When she touched him, his arm hung off the stretcher. Quickly, gently, she set it back. But when she took her hands away it fell again, limp, lifeless. She caught her breath as she lifted her son's arm a second time and held it on the stretcher.

"Something popped out in his neck," Gilbert said quietly. "They want to take him to Nashville but he ought to be okay. They don't think it's anything to worry about."

After some time, she had no idea how long, they moved Terry out to the ambulance and drove him down the short hill to the common area in front of Ray Hall. There on the lawn, a makeshift "X" had been prepared on the grass for the helicopter landing.

It was just after 7 p.m. and darkness had already settled on the campus. From inside the ambulance, Myrna looked out, wishing she knew more, then wishing she didn't. The lights from a dozen cars were aimed at the "X" and beside the cars she could see groups of people huddled together, the steam from their breath forming clouds between them as they talked. What were they saying? Was Terry going to be all right?

Gilbert was back at the door of the ambulance with Ron Case, the Wilks family physician and a close personal friend. "We can't tell how serious it is yet," Ron was saying. "The doctor in Nashville will be able to tell more. I understand they've contacted Dr. Cushman, which is good. He's one of the best neurosurgeons in town."

Myrna gripped Terry's arm and nodded at Ron.

"We'll be down first thing in the morning," Ron told her. "Fred's coming down with Gilbert, so he'll be with you tonight."

They could hear the helicopter in the distance now, drawing closer.

* * *

By now the pain was unbearable. Everytime they moved

him or touched him it rocked through his body. He had tried to fight it, but he had no fight left. Not for this much pain. "Please, God, just let me black out," he prayed.

He opened his eyes and Jonetta was leaning over him, smiling, patting his arm. Terry wanted to take her hand, but there was no response in his own. He winked at her and smiled. Despite the incredible pain, Terry was still smiling.

Another wave of pain and then he heard the familiar voice of his father. "They're going to move you now, Terry."

His head throbbed like a thumb hit by a hammer as they carried him the short distance to the craft and strapped his stretcher in.

"Please, God, please let me black out," he prayed again as the vibrations from the helicopter drove the level of pain beyond what he could endure.

"Mom," he cried.

There was no answer. Again he called for his mother, and again there was no answer. Terry opened his eyes to darkness.

"Mom!"

"I'm right here, Terry," Myrna said finally. He looked in the direction of her voice, but he could see nothing. She was touching his leg, but he couldn't feel it. She held him as the others moved back from the landing area.

"Please, God. . . ." he prayed again and as the helicopter lifted off Terry finally blacked out, his pain merging with the pulsating whir of the propeller.

* * *

Gilbert stared at the bright glow from his headlights as he aimed his car into the darkness of Interstate 65. Fred Curry was beside him in the front seat, and in the backseat, Terry's sister, Diane, and her friend, Rhonda Watts, sat in silence.

'Terry's going to be okay,' Gilbert said to himself. 'But why did it happen? Why Terry? Of all people, he deserves to suffer the least. Why would God let something like this happen? Is he trying to punish me? He couldn't be punishing Terry. Terry's done nothing wrong.

'But he's going to be okay. The doctor's probably going to pop something back in his neck and in two or three days, he'll be up and around again.'

"It's too bad Terry's going to miss the trip to Louisville," Gilbert said to Fred. "He always has such a good time on those road trips. I think they're really good for the kids, don't you?"

Fred nodded but said nothing. Fred had seen the Xrays, Gilbert knew. He wanted to ask Fred how it looked but he couldn't yet. They'd find out when they got to Nashville.

After a moment, Gilbert spoke again.

"You saw it," he said. "The accident, I mean."

"Yes, I did," Fred said.

"What exactly happened?"

As Fred described it in general terms, Gilbert could see his son's head being pressed back against his back. The vision was very clear in his mind. But how far back? How severely had his neck been bent? That was the question Gilbert wanted to ask, but he couldn't.

"Why was he trying something so hard?" Gilbert asked and Fred could only shrug.

Gilbert felt a sickening weight in his stomach. Maybe he'd pushed Terry too hard. Maybe it was HIS fault.

* * *

As they turned into the Memorial Hospital parking lot, Diane pointed to the helicopter sitting idle now on the darkened landing pad. They hurried into the emergency room and immediately saw Myrna at the admitting desk, talking to a nurse.

"Thank goodness," she said as Gilbert appeared at her side.

There were insurance questions to answer. While he took care of that, Myrna went to be with Diane.

"You got here so fast," she said. Diane was shivering. "Where's your coat?"

Diane only shrugged and shivered some more.

"What was the helicopter like?"

"It was all right," Myrna said. "The landing was hard but Terry had passed out."

Diane cringed. "What's wrong with him?" she asked, holding herself to keep from shaking. "Why doesn't anybody say what's wrong with him?"

"They don't know yet," Myrna replied.

* * *

"Mr. and Mrs. Wilks?"

"Yes," Gilbert said, standing up. He had just finished leading the others in prayer.

The nurse asked him to step into the hall. "Dr. Cushman is ready to see you," the nurse said. "Dr. Cushman is pretty straight. It may sound rough when he says it, but he knows what he's talking about. Just listen to him."

Gilbert and Myrna went back in to tell the others, and then Dr. Cushman walked in. His expression was sincere and compassionate. He didn't mince words.

"Terry has a dislocation of the spine. His spinal cord is severed or severely damaged between the fourth and fifth vertebrae. He has no response in his arms and legs, no strength or tone in his rectum. There's a ninety percent chance he's going to stay this way."

He paused, then continued.

"We've attached tongs and connected weights to try to reduce the fracture. If that doesn't work, surgery will be required."

Myrna and Diane hugged each other as tears stung their

eyes. Terry was paralyzed. The doctor hadn't used the word, but she knew that's what he meant.

Gilbert nodded at the doctor, trying to take in what he'd said. 'A ninety percent chance he would stay this way. That meant 10 percent made it. Terry could be in that 10 percent. Besides, doctors always paint a dark picture so you won't get your hopes up. Terry could still be up and around in a few days. It was still possible.'

* * *

Gilbert and Myrna walked down the hall and through the double doors into the emergency room. There, encased in a Stryker frame, was their son. The sight of him was shocking. What looked like ice tongs were clamped to the sides of his head. Actually the tongs were attached to two screws that had been drilled into his skull. A cable connected the tongs to some weights that hung off the head of the bed. The area around the screws was hairless and red from blood and iodine.

"Hey, Terry," Gilbert said, forcing himself to smile. Terry opened his eyes, but showed no recognition. Myrna reached over and stroked Terry's forehead and Gilbert quietly excused himself.

He walked stiffly down the hall to the men's room and stumbled inside. "God, this isn't so," he cried, falling against the cold tile wall. "What can I do?" The tears burst over his cheeks and clouded his glasses. He tried to collect himself, taking his glasses off and wiping them with a paper towel. As he did, he saw again his son with the tongs connected to his head, and his body shook convulsively. For minutes he wept out of control, before he made himself stop. He couldn't let Myrna or Terry see him cry. He had to be strong for them.

* * *

Terry felt a new wave of pain and parted his eyes. He was moving again. "We're taking you to ICU," a voice from behind said to him. He tried to smile in response. What was expected of him? How was he supposed to act? They stopped, then continued through a new set of double doors and Terry heard the sounds of new voices. He felt them turn his stretcher and back it up until finally they stopped.

"Terry?"

He opened his eyes to see a pretty, dark haired nurse, smiling at him. "I'm Kathy," she said. "You're in intensive care now. We're going to look after you here. I just need to ask you a few questions."

The questions had to do with his body. What could he feel? What could he move?

"Can you move your right foot?"

Nothing happened.

"Left foot."

It MOVED.

"Wonderful," Kathy said, and Terry's hopes surged.

"Right hand," she said, and again nothing happened. The same with the left hand.

But he had moved his foot. It was a sign of hope.

When the questions stopped, Terry began to think about his body, still fighting off the pain. It felt like his body was asleep, the same way his arm sometimes got when he slept on it wrong. There was a buzzing numbness where his arm was supposed to be. That's the way his body felt now.

Kathy began to make him comfortable, placing his hands and arms on boards covered with sheepskin and elevating his hands on towels, then putting white thigh-length stockings on each of his legs.

"Just try to relax," she said, but Terry could not relax. He could only think of death. It felt so close. And it was getting closer, everytime he had to fight for another breath.

He'd begged for medicine when he first arrived at the

hospital, but now he didn't want to go to sleep again, because if he did, he knew he would die. He saw himself in a casket, with his parents and friends standing over him. What did they think of him, now that he was gone? The thought made him open his eyes.

"It's okay," Kathy said, smiling.

"I'm afraid to go to sleep," he gasped.

"We're right here," she said. "You go on to sleep and if anything happens, we'll take care of you."

He closed his eyes thankfully and she covered him with a blanket.

* * *

The weekend was torturous. Terry's pain reached its peak Friday afternoon and there it remained. Despite Gilbert's pleas for more medication, the doctors assured him that Terry's dosage had to be kept at a low level because he needed all of his strength to keep breathing. The pain was something he would have to endure until they had stabilized the area around the injury.

On Saturday, Dr. Cushman informed Gilbert that the traction was not having the desired effect of pulling the vertebrae apart. One vertebra had hooked over the other. They would have to surgically realign the vertebrae and wire them together. But Dr. Cushman was not as concerned about the surgery as the swelling that would follow.

Terry was already having a hard time breathing. The injury had left all of the muscles used for breathing paralyzed except his diaphragm. However, after surgery, the swelling around the spinal cord could cut off the nerves to the diaphragm as well.

"He's going to have to fight hard," Dr. Cushman told Gilbert. "But he seems to be a fighter."

* * *

When Dr. Cushman told Terry he would have surgery on Monday, Terry cried tears of joy. He had prayed for something to ease the pain. Maybe surgery would do it. 'I must stay alive until Monday,' Terry told himself, fighting his exhaustion. 'I can last that long.'

Fighting to breathe and fighting the pain were enough to consume him, without the fear he had to fight each time they turned him on the Stryker frame. The canvas sheets were stretched tight to cover him on top and bottom so they could turn him face down at regular intervals to keep his blood flowing properly. About four inches separated the top from the bottom at the outer edges, and everytime they turned him, Terry had a fear of sliding through the crack. Once he almost did, when the frame got stuck in mid-turn.

By the end of the weekend, Terry had lost all sense of physical dignity. He had no control. On Sunday afternoon, while he was turned on his stomach, one of the IV catheters connected on his arm came loose, and suddenly blood was spurting onto the floor. Terry watched it with an exhausted detachment.

"Hey, nurse, look at this," he said as if something unusual had just come on TV. It didn't scare him because he couldn't FEEL it. It was as if it wasn't his blood at all.

* * *

Finally, at noon on Monday, they informed Terry that it was time to prepare for surgery. He was wheeled to the prep room, full of hope. He didn't know what the surgery would do, but he knew it had to make him better because he couldn't get worse.

The anesthetist came in to put him to sleep and suddenly

Terry's mind was racing with a thousand thoughts. How long would he have to stay in the hospital? When could he go home to his friends, go back to school? When could he be NORMAL again?

"I'm going to put this mask over your face and I want you to breathe real deep."

Tears of frustration filled Terry's eyes. "I can't breathe deep," he whispered. "I just. . . ."

The mask covered his face and a heavy blanket of sleep descended over him. It was his first release from pain since he'd blacked out on the helicopter ride from Portland.

* * *

Terry felt himself rising to the surface again, as if he were under water, straining those final few seconds before his head broke through and he could breathe again. He labored to catch the first breath and opened his eyes. He was alone in the recovery room. Where was everybody? What had happened? He struggled to breathe again and relaxed back into the darkness he'd come from.

Then he was rising again, holding his breath, moving. He was moving. Was he in the hall? Things began to go black again, then there was a faint light. He opened his eyes and could see the blurry images of people standing over him.

"Terry, it's Mom." Myrna and Dr. Case walked beside the stretcher as Terry was wheeled back to the intensive care unit.

Terry felt himself going under again. He couldn't grab any air. He tried to take a breath and this time, nothing happened. "No air," he blurted.

He could hear the sounds of sudden shouting as he felt himself going back under. 'I'm going to bust. I'm dying.'

As he descended into the darkness, he saw his death. 'Mom's going to be crying in a minute,' he said to himself. 'After I die...in the twinkling of an eye. I'll see Christ coming. It's all right. I can go.'

Terry was in a golden cave, floating, coasting in a soft haze of consciousness. But as he continued to float, he began to feel unsettled. What else was there? was he supposed to see God? 'Don't tell me this is it,' he said. 'After all I've done to try to be what God wanted me to be, don't tell me I'm not going to have my reward in heaven. Where is God?'

"Terry!"

The sound was not what he was expecting. It was coming from someplace outside. Where was God? Then he heard the voice again, this time louder, closer. 'Maybe I'm not dead.'

"It's okay, he's stabilizing."

Then he realized he was breathing again. He was still alive.

"Terry?"

He opened his eyes. His mother was crying, and Dr. Case was beside her, looking down at him.

"I thought I was dead," he said weakly.

"And you thought you were in heaven, but when you heard my voice you knew you couldn't be," Dr. Case replied.

Everyone laughed, thankful for a break in the tension. Terry managed to smile, but he couldn't help thinking about his close call.

They had rescued him before he had died. Terry closed his eyes, already returning to that semiconsciousness, where the pain was at least at a distance.

* * *

Dr. Cushman's eyes again showed concern.

"We were unable to reduce the fracture with traction so we performed an open reduction. In other words, we made an incision in the back of the neck, went down to the spine and physically relocated the fracture and wired it together. Then we took some bone from his hip and fused that in to help stabilize the injury."

"So then. . .what? Will his breathing be okay? Will he get more movement back?"

"There's a possibility that swelling of the cord after surgery may affect his breathing. Then he'll need a respirator. We'll know that within the next several days. As for his movement, sometimes they do improve and get a little movement back below the injury, and sometimes they don't. There's no way to detect in his particular case whether he will or not."

* * *

In the days following his surgery, Terry resumed the torturous struggle to fight the pain in his head and breathe. His lungs and stomach began to fill with mucous that he was unable to cough up, because of the swelling around his spinal cord. Ice packs were placed on both sides of his neck. A tube had been inserted through Terry's nose into his stomach to feed him and another tube ran into his trachea, to suction the mucous collecting there. They had placed Terry in the isolation unit at the end of the ward, so he and his family could have as much privacy as possible. But with each passing day, Terry grew weaker.

On Thursday morning, Terry was alone in the isolation unit. He had been turned onto his stomach for his regular back treatment and had complained of feeling nauseous. Kathy Smith had come in and was standing beside him, monitoring his breathing, when Terry began coughing up a thick gray substance. She jumped at the sound, moving faster than normal, not because the sound was loud, but because it was so weak.

"Call respiratory therapy quick," she yelled to Montry, the head nurse. "Get Cushman. We're going to lose him if we don't get help fast."

Kathy picked up the telephone. "Code 99," she said. "Code 99 in ICU."

In the waiting room, Myrna was startled by the piercing sound of an alarm. She looked up as three attendants dashed down the hall into the intensive care unit.

She stood up instinctively. 'Is it Terry?' she asked no one.

Don't worry, she told herself. It's probably not Terry. It could be any of a hundred different things.

Terror filled Terry's eyes. His skin was a sickly yellow-gray. He was doing all he could to breathe. The nurses couldn't bend his head back to hyper-extend his neck because of the fracture. They needed to get an air tube into his lungs immediately. If they couldn't insert it through his mouth, they would have to cut a hole in his throat.

"He's in pain," Montry said. "Ten cc's of codeine."

In frantic discussion, the half dozen nurses, therapists and anesthesiologists agreed. Terry needed a tracheotomy, immediately.

"Help me," Terry mouthed the words in desperation.

"We're gonna get you some air," Montry answered. "Hang on."

Terry blacked out. "Pulse is 36," someone whispered.

Montry trembled with fear, then she took a deep breath of hope as Dr. Classen, the chief anesthesiologist, hurried in, followed by Dr. Cushman.

"Prepare the trach tray," Cushman said immediately and the staff moved into action, but before the tray was ready, Dr. Classen had delicately slid a tube down Terry's throat through his mouth. The swelling made the process a slow and painstaking one, but finally she maneuvered the tube into Terry's trachea. She connected the tube to the respirator and Terry was breathing again.

"Start another IV," Dr. Cushman said and Montry slid the needle in and started atropine. A minute later, his pulse was up to 60. "Thank God," Kathy whispered.

In the waiting room Myrna had been unable to return to her needlepoint after the alarm sounded. Despite her repeated assurances to herself that it wasn't Terry, she wanted desperately to know what had happened. When Montry came through the double doors, Myrna looked up apprehensively.

"Now don't worry," Montry said. "He's all right."

Myrna jumped up. "It WAS Terry."

"He's okay. Everything's under control. We were lucky we had the right people here when we needed them."

Myrna felt cold with fear as Montry described the ordeal.

"He got a mucous plug in his throat and couldn't breathe. Dr. Classen was able to get a tube down his throat and now he's breathing fine. He just needs to rest right now." She patted Myrna's arm. "We were very lucky that Dr. Classen was in the hospital. You folks must be living right because God was sure on your side."

Terry was out of it that night. They had given him a large dose of codeine. The tube down his throat was connected to a respirator, which was pumping air into his lungs. As long as he was connected to the respirator, he would not have to worry about breathing. But the tube in his mouth would have to be removed, and a tracheotomy performed, so the tube could be inserted directly into his windpipe.

The next morning, Montry came in to see how he had fared during the night. He was weak, but still managed a smile.

"You're going to need this machine for a while," she said, pointing to the respirator. "It's giving you air. It's good for you."

Terry looked groggily at the respirator. What difference did it make? Even if the machine was bad, he couldn't do anything about it. He thought about his lifeless arms, connected by plastic tubes to the bottles of pain-killing fluids that were flowing into his body. On the side of his bed was a "bed bag," where his amber colored urine collected. He didn't even know when he urinated anymore. He was alive, but that was all.

* * *

It was Saturday night and Terry was resting quietly. Gilbert sat beside the bed, trying to collect himself. The sight of the tongs connected to Terry's head still left him with a numbing fear. His life had been so pain free. How could something so painful happen to his first born son.

His life had been turned upside down. He hadn't been to work in a week. All of the energy and attention he'd focused on his business was now directed to this room, and his son lying lifeless on a canvas sheet.

For a week, he had forced himself to hold onto hope and be strong for his whole family, and everyday it seemed things got worse, not better. After the Code 99 scare, Dr. Cushman had explained to him the need for a tracheostomy. Terry's vital signs were still strong, but he would have to remain in intensive care until everything had stabilized. In the meantime, his breathing was their primary concern.

The doctor suggested that Gilbert visit another patient who had suffered the same injury five years before and recently had returned to the hospital because of breathing problems. Gilbert went, hoping to be encouraged, but what he saw did just the opposite. Five years after his accident, the young man still depended on a respirator, at least part of the time, to stay alive. Would the same be true for Terry? How could his son live such an existence, after a life that was so full and active? How could God let this happen?

Gilbert thought back to the fun times of their life. He remembered Enterprise, Kansas in 1968. Terry was six that year and Diane was four, and they lived in a small house across from the town park, not far from the academy where Gilbert and Myrna had first met twelve years before. Gilbert was 29 and had just started his new business, printing television guides for small towns in Missouri and Arkansas. The possibilities of the business seemed limitless to him and his energy seemed inexhaustible.

Terry was the same way, a go-getter even then. Always doing something. Gilbert remembered how he had loved taking his sister to the swings in the park or on adventures into the woods behind their house.

Gilbert thought about all the times—it seemed like every Saturday—that he had to take Terry out of church and spank him for talking during the service. He had always done his best to make Terry understand what the spankings were for, and hugged him when they were over to let him know how much he loved him. But in the quiet of the hospital room, he could feel the sting of those spankings as if they'd just been administered.

Gilbert sighed and wondered how he would ever live with the memories. He looked at the bed bag attached to the bed and thought about the days when Terry was still a baby in diapers. He could remember when Terry was almost four and Myrna had told Terry she would give him a nickel for every night he didn't wet the bed.

Terry had broken the habit in a week.

He'd gone to work for Gilbert's press at age eight, sweeping the floor for $5 a week. When he was twelve he had enough money to buy his first horse, Sheba. Gilbert thought about what a sight it had been to watch his son galloping across the pasture behind their new home in Portland, slapping Sheba on the sides, urging her to go faster. She never went fast enough for Terry.

He'd bought that horse because of a girl, Gilbert remembered. Her name was Rondee. She was a tomboy all the way; raised on a boy's dude ranch in Nebraska by her parents, never without her cowboy boots, even when she wore a dress to school. She was a cute girl and he remembered how they used to tease him about marrying Rondee.

Terry had seemed to grow up a lot that year. Gilbert could remember the serious look on his son's face when he came to him one night after supper. "Dad," he'd said. "I've decided I want to be an architect when I grow up. Either that or an engineer."

Gilbert opened his eyes, almost ashamed for allowing himself the memories, but he couldn't help it. They were TRUE. His son had been an exceptional boy, and that made it all the harder to accept anything bad.

But what had pushed him to try to be so perfect all the time? Where had that tendency come from? Gilbert didn't know, but he could remember the first time he noticed it. It was right at that same time—when he had his crush on Rondee.

Terry had decided to paint a picture of a horse and give it to Rondee for her birthday. He'd been very excited to start on the project, but as he worked on it, the project began to consume him. He wouldn't allow a line to be out of place. It had to be perfect. He kept working on it and kept working on it until Gilbert had finally demanded that he give the picture to Rondee, and still Terry insisted on a few final changes.

From then, he'd noticed the tendency in dozens of different ways. In school and sports and even at work. Terry seemed to labor over everything until it was perfect, no matter how menial the task, nor how long it took. What was it that had made him do that?

Gilbert rubbed his forehead, thinking about his own youth. When he was in those early teenage years, he'd gone through a change himself but for him it had been more black and white.

He'd come from a poor family in Garden City, Kansas. His mother was a willful, Christian woman, and his father had been a true craftsman before he turned to alcohol. Gilbert had grown up with the same kind of love for action that his son had, but for him, that energy began to translate itself more and more into anti-social behavior. Gilbert became more unruly until finally, at age 14, he was kicked out of high school.

The change in his life had occurred right before he was expelled. He had been lying in bed one night and suddenly his sins began flashing before his eyes. Gilbert became convinced he would die that night. He had to get his sins forgiven. He was going to die and he wanted to be right with God.

At midnight, he ran to the dean's apartment. "I'm going to die tonight," he said. "I have to make my sins right, but it's too late." The dean quieted his fears and assured him that God had heard his prayers and everything was going to be all right.

The next day, he began going to people and asking for forgiveness. That began the process. When Gilbert returned to school the following year, he was a changed person. He had come to a choice between good and bad and he'd chosen good.

Now as he looked at Terry, he wondered if he had pushed too hard to make sure his son made the same choice. Maybe it was his fault that Terry had been hurt. But if it was his fault, then why wasn't he the one who was injured? Why was it Terry who had to suffer?

As he looked at Terry, he recalled a conversation he'd had that morning with a friend from the Highland community, who was trying, like Gilbert, to find some sense in the accident.

"If it had to happen to somebody, it's better that it happened to Terry, because no one else could have handled it as well as he has."

Gilbert had said nothing at the time, but the words had hurt him badly. Why did it have to happen at all? And, if Terry's such a neat kid, why him? He had so much to give in so many other ways, why would God allow him to use all of his energy and strength just to fight pain? It was such a waste.

As Gilbert sat in the stiff, uncomfortable chair beside Terry's Stryker frame, he felt death all around him. Two nights earlier, Gilbert had met a very nice woman whose husband had been admitted with a stroke. They talked about the shock of suddenly seeing a loved one disabled, especially one who was active and healthy, like her husband had been. The following morning, she was informed that her husband had died during the night.

Gilbert had cried with her and thanked the Lord that it hadn't been Terry. That same day, another patient had been brought into ICU and placed in the bed beside Terry's. He had been injured in a car accident and was in a coma. He was only 22 years old. The nurses knew him from previous hospital stays and they were angry that he had been involved in another accident—he'd been drunk and driven his car into a utility pole—but Gilbert could only think about his future. Would he ever regain consciousness, and if he did, what would his life be like?

The heaviness he felt in his chest had become a permanent condition it seemed. All of his life he had prided himself on being in control and now things were totally out of his control. There was nothing he could do. He had to trust the Lord to take care of his son.

Gilbert looked at his briefcase leaning against the wall. He'd brought it with him so he could get some work done, but he'd been unable to concentrate on it. The business was running itself now, something he couldn't have even imagined a week before. Despite all the appearances of prosperity, Wilks Publications was operating in the red, and had been for several months. Gilbert had made the decision to expand into a number of new markets in the past year, and now that expansion had caught up with him. Sales in the new markets were going slower than he'd projected, and the overhead at his two plants in Tennessee and Oregon was driving the company further in debt. He was going to have to borrow thousands of the bank to get through the next several months, and he knew if the bank saw the coming month's balance sheet the loan might be turned down.

But now, none of that mattered. The business didn't matter. If Terry could recover and the family could be together again, then he could find a way to make a living.

Gilbert thought about the trip to Oregon he'd planned for himself, Myrna, David and his private, part-time pilot. They were to have left the morning after Terry's accident, first to Dallas where Gilbert planned to discuss problems with one of his salesmen, then to Oregon where he was going to close the plant. Gilbert was a pilot himself and he had been concerned about going through the Rockies in their single-engine Bonanza. Since the accident, he'd learned that there had been severe snow storms that day along the route they'd charted. If Terry hadn't been injured and they'd taken the trip, maybe they'd have been the ones. . . .

"But why did it have to be Terry?" he cried to himself, wishing more than anything that he could trade places with his son.

Suddenly Gilbert jumped at a noise close beside him. He turned quickly to see the young man in the next bed sitting up. He started to stand and Gilbert jumped up with his fists clenched, as the man stumbled towards Terry's bed.

"I've got to go to the bathroom," he mumbled. Gilbert was ready to shove the man back into bed if he came any closer. "One of the patients is up!" he shouted.

A nurse hurried in and steadied the man, leading him toward the bathroom and Gilbert finally sat back down shaking.

For two days the man had lain silently in the next bed, more detached from life even than Terry. Now, miraculously, he had recovered, right before Gilbert's eyes. A man who had been out joyriding, endangering the lives of others, suddenly healed, while his son lay paralyzed. How could God explain it? And how could he accept it?

* * *

The tracheotomy was performed the following Tuesday morning and Terry was able to relax a little more. He wasn't having to fight for every breath now, though the respirator was set at eight breaths a minute, which meant he still had to work.

He needed the respirator, he knew, but with the tube in his throat, he couldn't talk.

What would be next, he wondered? He couldn't move. He couldn't eat. He couldn't breathe. And now he couldn't talk. What good was he? He was nothing more than a machine that was being manipulated—kept alive—by others. When people came to visit, the only way he could interact with them was to smile. But could he keep smiling?

At least now, they were giving him medicine for the pain. The demerol and codeine allowed him to relax more, but it also dulled his brain. He was without emotion. Every ounce of energy he had was dedicated to fighting the pain and staying alive, and he had nothing left to give, even to the people—like Mike Parks—who were keeping him alive.

Mike was the respiratory therapist in charge of monitoring Terry's respirator and breathing regularity. He was one of the few people who seemed relaxed and able to be himself around Terry.

"I remember you," he'd said the first day they met. "I was here the night you came in. I saw the chopper land and everything."

Terry smiled.

"You came in on a Huey, probably from the 507th MEDEVAC at Fort Campbell. I used to be stationed up there, right next door to that unit. Small world, isn't it?"

Terry liked Mike and began to look forward to his visits. One day they were kidding around and Mike made him laugh so hard the bed shook. Later outside, Mike stopped Gilbert and apologized. "I don't want to hurt the guy," he said.

Gilbert shook his head. "Please don't stop," he said. "Laughter's the best medicine."

As much as Terry liked Mike, however, he hated the reason for his visits.

Every two hours, Mike or one of the nurses came in to clean out the tubes and insert medication to break up the mucous that had formed in Terry's lungs. The respirator was disconnected and an airbag attached to his trach hole. By pumping the airbag, they filled Terry's lungs with air.

Then the difficult part began. The airbag was removed and a suction tube inserted and as Terry began to cough, the suction tube removed the mucous collecting in Terry's lungs. The nurses helped by pounding on his chest to force the air out and help dislodge the mucous. And someone, quite often Gilbert, was asked to watch the mucous as it passed through a clear tube, to be sure it contained no blood.

The process took about thirty minutes, and when it was over, Terry was exhausted. But there wasn't time enough to sleep, because two hours later, they would be back to do it again.

Since the day after his first operation, Terry had been unable to hold down solid foods. He'd been fed through a tube for three weeks and the lining of his stomach was becoming ulcerated from the cortisone they were giving him. He needed solid foods.

* * *

On Friday night Terry finally took his first bites of food and held it down. It was an orange that Kathy had brought him, and he ate a third of it. That night Terry had one of his best nights sleeping since he'd entered the hospital. He woke up the next morning, ready for a good breakfast.

They fed him at 9 a.m. By noon he was complaining of nausea. He was given medication but continued vomiting throughout the afternoon By six o'clock his temperature was 102 degrees, and although he was still vomiting, his stomach had swelled up like the belly of a woman who was nine months pregnant.

Gilbert had been with Terry in the early afternoon but had left for several hours. When he returned he immediately knew Terry was in trouble. He yelled for a nurse and Tom ran into the room.

"We've got to suction his stomach," Tom said. He grabbed an NG tube and inserted it in Terry's nose.

"Swallow, Terry," he commanded as Terry felt the tube covered with slimy jelly at his throat. "Swallow!"

Tears rushed down the sides of Terry's face as he forced himself to swallow the tube. Slowly at first, and then in a gush, the mucous drained from his stomach. In the next thirty minutes, Tom pumped out almost two quarts of liquid and an equal amount of air.

When it was finally over, Tom reached down and patted Terry's stomach. "Well, we made it through another one, buddy."

Terry's eyes were filled with gratitude. He nodded and smiled at Tom.

* * *

Tom sat at the nurses' station with his supervisor, Montry. It was the beginning of Monday's shift and he was telling her about Terry's weekend ordeal.

"It was awful," Tom said. "He was so full he was

overflowing. And scared to death. But the weirdest part was that when it was all over, he smiled."

Montry nodded. "Sometimes I wonder if he realizes how bad off he really is."

Tom shook his head. "I don't think he realizes it, and I think that might be bad for him in the long run. The longer he goes without knowing what his condition is, the harder it's going to be for him when he finds out."

Montry shrugged. "I'll talk to Dr. Cushman."

That afternoon, Montry took Cushman aside after his rounds, and told him what she and Tom had discussed.

"We think it might be better if he knew what he was up against," she said. "I'm afraid he thinks he's going to return to normal when this is all over."

Cushman shook his head. "Not now," he said. "Whatever hope he's got, he needs to keep it up until he stabilizes. He needs all the courage he can get. When he gets through this, then we'll let him face reality."

* * *

Myrna took a deep breath as she pulled out of the apartment complex parking lot and headed toward the hospital. It had been almost a month now and the routine was taking its toll. She had never considered herself a strong person and she'd surprised herself with her strength through this ordeal, but she didn't know how long she could keep it up.

Dr. Cushman had told them that if Terry continued to stabilize, he would be able to move out of intensive care on the following Thursday, March 19. Exactly one month after the accident. It seemed like a year when she thought about all of the battles they'd fought that month, but when she thought about Terry it seemed like the accident had been yesterday. She could still see him, jogging out to the car that morning with his books under his arm. So strong and confident.

As she waited at a stoplight, she heard the sound of an ambulance behind her and she waited until it had passed. 'I wonder what happened?' she thought. 'I wonder who those people are? How will it affect the family?' She felt an identity with the people in the ambulance that she could never have felt before. Their lives would never be the same.

As Myrna walked into the ICU, Mike Parks was just coming through the door.

"Hey," he said, "I hear they're moving Terry a step down."

Myrna nodded. "I hope you'll still be taking care of him."

"Sure. I wouldn't let anybody else take care of my buddy. He'll be on the respirator for a couple more weeks at least until the swelling goes down enough that he can start breathing on his own again."

"Yes, we're very happy he's going to be able to come off the respirator."

Mike smiled at her. "It's not going to be easy, Mrs. Wilks. Terry needs the respirator. His diaphragm muscle isn't having to work. When he goes off the respirator, it's going to be very hard for him to get it working again. That can be the toughest fight of all. But don't worry, we'll be with him. He's hung in there this long. He's going to make it."

When Myrna sat down beside Terry, the conversation was playing through her mind. "That can be the toughest fight of all. . . ." She leaned over and began massaging Terry's forehead, her eyes drawn to the respirator. It had been such a welcome aid for the past few weeks—and suddenly she felt distrustful. Terry was going to have to free himself of that machine. What had been a friend was now an enemy.

As she rubbed his head, she noticed again how frail he was and she thought of a Bible verse she'd read several nights before. She often read to Terry at night. Sometimes the Bible, sometimes other books he liked. That had become a special time for them, one of the few times she saw any signs of peacefulness in Terry's face. That night, she'd read the 12th chapter of John. The chapter recounted an episode in which Jesus was challenged by doubters to explain his references to his own impending death.

He replied: "Yet a little while is the light with you. Walk while ye have the light, lest darkness come upon you: for he that walketh in darkness knoweth not whither he goeth."

The verse had made her think of Terry, "Walk while ye have the light. . . ." If anyone had the light, she believed it was Terry. Yet he couldn't walk. The pain of it went into her heart.

Myrna's LIFE was her children. She could remember the times of their childhood in vivid detail: Terry running around clad only in his diaper when they lived in Elizabethtown while Gilbert was in the Army; watching Terry and Diane running through the fruit trees at Grandpa's, how they loved being outside. She also remembered a time of depression in her own life, when it had been thoughts of her children that brought her out of it.

Now, as she looked down at her oldest son, she felt so helpless. Terry was in so much pain and no one could take it away from him. When she thought of how much he hurt, she remembered the worst pain she'd ever experienced. It was the pain of Terry's birth.

"Lord," she prayed. "Please make him whole again."

We
Had
Hope

The pall that hung over the hospital room in Nashville was almost as oppressive in Portland, Tennessee, thirty miles to the north. For the members of the tight-knit Highland community, Terry Wilks was one of their children and his injury was a family crisis.

From the beginning the community had turned all of its spiritual energy to Terry's recovery. On Monday of his first surgery, there were people in the church praying for Terry from 6 a.m. until midnight. Small prayer groups were formed among his classmates, and almost everyday a group of students drove into Memorial Hospital. Sometimes they weren't allowed in to see him but they stayed anyway, trying to comfort his family and each other.

The outpouring of love for Terry amazed the Memorial Hospital staff. He received so many get-well cards that the people in the mail room began asking if Terry Wilks was a Grand Ole Opry entertainer.

During the first week everyone's hopes had remained high, but everyday brought bad news from Nashville. The constant pain, his near death after surgery, Code 99. They prayed for God's blessing on their friend, and every day the news was worse.

Then the insurance men came. They spent several days on campus interviewing the principal, the coach and the other members of the gymnastics team, and when they left, spirits sunk to a new low. Who was legally responsible for the accident? The question seemed cold and insignificant when they considerd the bigger question: "Why Terry?"

The longer he was in pain, the harder it was to accept. It was especially hard on Robbie Elliott, who visited Terry's room one night when he was feeling especially down.

It had been a bad day for Terry as well. His last ventilator check had been very long and painful. The mucous in his lungs was thick and had to be diluted with saline solution, and the nurse had pounded on his chest to break up the congestion until he begged her to leave him alone so he could sleep.

When Robbie arrived, Terry managed a smile. Robbie talked to him about school activities. Spring break was the following week and everyone was getting ready for the school ski trip to Winter Park, Colorado. They had considered cancelling the trip because of Terry, but he insisted they go.

"I don't even want to go if you're not going to be there," Robbie said. "Sometimes I see you just getting up out of that bed and walking out of here. I really think that can happen, Terry, if we believe it hard enough. If our faith is strong enough."

Robbie asked Terry to pray with him and when he left that night he told Terry he was going to wait by the telephone in the lobby. "If it's God's will, you'll get up and call me down there. I'll be waiting."

When Robbie left the room, Terry closed his eyes and thought about the telephone. How much he would give to be able to pick it up and talk to Robbie. But then he thought about his next breathing treatment, less than an hour away. He couldn't dream about a miracle. All he could dream about was sleep.

As tired as he was, he still wanted his friends there. He needed them. Sometimes when he seemed barely able to go on, the arrival of a friend could transform him. Gilbert and Myrna saw it happen when Rosalie came down to cut his hair, and again when Jonetta arrived with banana nut bread she baked herself. The light would come back into his eyes, he would smile and everyone would feel better again.

The person who visited most often was Joanne, Terry's old girlfriend. Joanne had been in class when she heard of Terry's accident. She had burst into tears, left the classroom and driven to Nashville that afternoon to be near him. Almost everyday, Joanne came to the hospital, even when she knew she wouldn't be allowed in to see him. She just wanted to be close.

* * *

The bus made its way west through the cold Kansas night with its cargo of young passengers, on their way for a week of skiing in Winter Park, Colorado. In a seat by a window, Diane tried to get comfortable, pulling the blanket tighter around her. She couldn't sleep. So many thoughts crowded her mind, none of them pleasant.

It had been a difficult year. After 16 years of a secure and carefree life, everything had been thrown out of synch. Her brother, a stable and important part of her life, like her parents, had suddenly been taken away from her.

How could this happen to her brother? He was such a nice person. If Terry could be hurt so badly for no reason, then nothing seemed secure to her. She thought about how much time the two of them had spent together growing up. All of the wonderful afternoon rides through the woods on their horses, making up cowboy games, chasing each other across the big pasture.

And now Terry was in a hospital bed, struggling for his life. Diane realized that her parents had to be with Terry each day through his struggle, but their absence made her feel even more alone. Her security had been taken away and she didn't know if it would ever return.

She began to cry softly, trying not to let the others hear. Since her parents had moved into the apartment in Nashville to be close to Terry, she had stayed with several families in Portland. To them she was still the same friendly, smiling Diane. Her friends told her she acted like nothing had happened. She needed to let it out. But she didn't know what she felt or if she felt anything at all. She couldn't cry with her friends. So she waited until she was alone at night.

* * *

Terry opened his eyes and looked at the respirator beside him, pumping air into his lungs. The machine had become his constant companion, traveling with him from intensive care to intermediate care like a member of the family. He had wanted so much to be able to walk out of the intensive care unit under his own power, but now the thought of walking seemed like a distant dream. So did the thought of sleep. With the regular respiratory checks, Terry had begun to measure his life in two hour segments. What little strength he had left to fight was being drained from him by the constant interruptions. And when they weren't "airbagging" him, they were bathing him, turning him, checking his tubes or emptying his urine bag. It never seemed to stop and all of it was demoralizing, even the baths, because he stayed cold for so long afterwards.

At least the doctors were giving him pain medication for his headaches, but they'd told him that when the time came to take him off the respirator, the medication would have to be cut back as well so he would have all his strength to regain his ability to breathe.

Terry couldn't think about having to breathe on his own again. All he could think about was his overwhelming fatigue. Terry had begged them to let him sleep, but they told him he could catch pneumonia if the mucous was allowed to collect in his lungs. He would have to hang in there, but he didn't know how much longer he could do that.

* * *

Five days after Terry moved to intermediate care, Dr. Cushman announced that the swelling around his spinal cord had finally subsided, and the torturous process of weaning him from the respirator began.

Each day, Mike would come in and plug the "trach" hole in Terry's throat, letting him breathe on his own. On the first day, Terry had thought something must be wrong. He COULDN'T breathe. No matter how hard he tried, he couldn't get any air in his lungs. Surely they didn't mean for him to breathe on his own NOW. Maybe in a week or two, when he was at least a little stronger. But they wouldn't wait.

"Just do your best," Mike told him. "Try to get a breath."

Tears streamed down Terry's face. It was like trying to suck air from a milk jug. But he tried anyway, fighting to breathe until the whole bed shook from his effort.

And somehow, he made progress. Each day they left him off the machine a little longer.

"You can do it, buddy," Mike would say to him, smiling his encouragement. But Terry did not have the strength to smile back anymore.

* * *

Terry's eyes felt like hot light bulbs and his eyelids like sandpaper. When he looked at the visitor standing beside his bed, he felt like he was looking out through a screen of smoked glass. Nothing seemed real. It was as if he were dreaming.

"Hi, Terry, it's Dean Tucker. How you doing?"

"Okay." Terry mouthed the word. He couldn't talk because the respirator was connected.

"I'm going to be staying with you tonight. If you need anything just let me know."

"Okay," Terry said again.

"Great," Dean smiled.

When Terry closed his eyes, Dean took a deep breath. He had never been around anyone as sick as Terry was, and he wasn't at all sure what he should do. He had only been working for Wilks Publications a few months at the time of Terry's accident, so he wasn't as close to the family as the other people from Portland who came to the hospital to sit with him. But Dean and his wife, Kathy, had wanted to do something to help out, and when Gilbert told them he and Myrna were both exhausted, Dean quickly volunteered to spend a night with Terry, so they could get some rest. Gilbert was genuinely thankful. The whole Wilks family was feeling sick, and he was going to check them all into the emergency room to try and find out what they had. If it was a virus, they certainly didn't want to expose Terry to it. Not in his condition.

"Excuse me."

Dean turned and saw a friendly nurse.

"Will you be staying tonight?"

He nodded.

The nurse explained to Dean the procedures they would follow during the night.

"When we take him off the respirator, we push it out of the room because it's a psychological advantage for him to know he's breathing on his own. He is doing better all the time, especially at night. His breathing comes much easier when he's asleep. Tonight we're going to leave the respirator out and see if he can make it through the night without it. It may be tough for him but we'll be close by, in case anything happens."

She explained that the clips attached to Terry's sunken chest were connected to an apnea monitor which checked Terry's breathing. His respiration rate should not go over 40 and not drop below 20. If it went too high, a signal went off and the nurses would come in and check him.

By 2 a.m., Dean was having a hard time staying awake, but he couldn't keep his eyes off the apnea monitor. Around midnight, Terry's respiration count had climbed to 40, and Dean had sprung from his chair, but then it had dropped back to 36 and stayed there. Dean had relaxed, realizing that Terry had fallen asleep, but then the nurses came in for his ventilator check, suctioning mucous from his lungs, urging Terry to take deep breaths and attempt to cough up the mucous on his own.

When they left, Dean's heart went out to Terry. He was so exhausted.

The pattern continued throughout the night, and by morning, Terry was having a tougher time than usual breathing. When the nurses had left following the 6 a.m. ventilator check, Terry began gasping and turning his head frantically. Dean jumped from his chair. Terry's eyes were filled with terror.

"Help!" he whispered in what would have been a scream. "I can't take it anymore." His head rolled to the side.

Dean ran from the room and immediately there were nurses

rushing in. "I'll get the suction bag," one shouted, as another pushed the respirator in.

"Come on, Terry, breathe!" The nurse pounded on his chest, then opened his mouth to make sure he hadn't swallowed his tongue. "Please," she said, climbing on to the bed and cradling his head in her arms. "Please, God, don't let him go."

The respirator was pushed in and connected and finally air began passing into Terry's lungs again. Slowly Dean watched the terror drain from Terry's face as sleep returned.

"Thank God for that respirator," he said.

* * *

Gilbert awoke in the morning feeling better than he had in weeks. After receiving medication for his own minor illness, he'd finally gotten a good nights sleep. The doctor had told him it would be all right to pay Terry a short visit in the morning, and Gilbert was excited to see his son. He knew Terry had spent his first full night without the respirator. Maybe this would be the turning point.

As Gilbert passed the nurses' station, he smiled and said hello to everyone. He couldn't tell them how much he appreciated all they'd done. He was feeling so good and he wanted to share it with them. Maybe God hadn't performed the miracle he had hoped for, but that didn't mean God wouldn't perform a long-term miracle. Gilbert took a deep breath as he walked into Terry's room, his smile radiating confidence.

The sight of the respirator beside Terry's bed hit Gilbert like a fist in the stomach. He slumped against the door. Dean looked up at him.

"Oh, no," Gilbert almost cried. "Not. . . . That's the end of it. There's no way we can. . . . " The tears welled in his eyes.

"He went all night," Dean said. "It was so rough. They only

put him back on it an hour ago."

Gilbert wiped at his eyes. "It's like we're back at square one," he sighed. "Everything's going backwards."

"At least he's sleeping," Dean said.

Gilbert nodded. He wanted to find hope in something, but the problems seemed insurmountable. Then he thought about his cold. "I better go back outside," he said. "I don't want to give him any germs."

Gilbert sat in the front seat of his car, weeping openly. This was it. Another setback just when it seemed Terry was ready to break free of being so close to death. He wasn't going to make it. How could he? He was so weak.

Gilbert wiped his eyes. He just wanted to get away. How could he live with his son bound to a respirator? He shuddered. He had to get away. 'I have my credit card,' he thought. The Nashville Airport was a thirty-minute drive from the hospital. Where could he go? His passport was in one of the suitcases at the apartment. He could stop by and get some clothes and his toothbrush and things.

Gilbert's body jerked at the thought. He couldn't leave. The thought seemed suddenly horrible to him. But how could he face his life? How could he go on?

His prayers finally began to calm him. He had to have faith. He had to believe there was a reason for it, even as his mind argued that no reason was good enough—not for this much pain. He had to accept it.

Gilbert's tears had stopped and he'd decided to drive to a store and buy groceries for the week when a familiar car pulled into the parking lot. It was Ron Case. Gilbert waved at him and Ron walked over to the car.

Ron had spent as much time with the Wilkses as his medical practice would allow. He'd been in the operating room with Dr. Cushman on the afternoon of Terry's first surgery, and had spent a lot of time with Gilbert, discussing the medical realities of Terry's injury. He could tell from the puffiness around Gilbert's eyes that it had already been a rough morning.

"He's back on the respirator," Gilbert said. "I don't know, Ron, he just doesn't seem to have the strength to make it."

"How's he doing now?"

"He's sleeping. Dean Tucker's still in with him."

"Well, that's good." Ron sat down in the passenger seat and Gilbert told him of Terry's ordeal the night before.

"Are you heading back to the apartment?" Ron asked.

"No, I'm going to buy some groceries."

"Mind if I tag along?"

As they drove out of the parking lot, Ron asked Gilbert how HE was doing. Gilbert shook his head. "I just wish it was me in that bed instead of him. I want to be with him all the time, Ron. When I see him and talk to him and touch him, it's okay, but when I'm away from him and I think about what's happened. . ."

Gilbert had to stop.

"Why don't we drive around some," Ron said as they neared the grocery store. Gilbert nodded absent-mindedly and turned onto Gallatin Road, heading toward Nashville. "Gilbert, Terry's accident was not your fault. You can't take his place."

Gilbert shook his head. "But why did it happen? I think about the way Terry was. Always trying to be perfect. Driving himself to be better in everything he did. Did I make him that way? If he hadn't been pushing himself like that, he never would have tried a double flip."

"Terry did push himself, but that was just his natural drive."

Gilbert stared out at the traffic, thinking. "Like with his car. Terry never drove his car over 55 miles per hour, because that was the law. That was the rule. And I don't know, I just thought he was driving himself crazy trying to be so perfect, so I encouraged him to take it out and rev it up. See what it would do. I remember he came in one night and told me he'd gotten it up to 95. I thought, 'Hey, maybe his thing about being perfect is breaking a little.' Then since the accident, I can't help thinking that if I hadn't done that, maybe Terry would have been more cautious about things and wouldn't have tried that flip."

"You're going to drive yourself crazy thinking like that. You can't take the blame for this. You are a good father, Gilbert. And you have to be a father now. You can't get inside Terry's skin and take his pain away from him. You can only do what you can to make his life easier."

Gilbert nodded looking out at the road. He knew Ron was right, but he couldn't get the thoughts out of his mind. It helped talking about it though. He'd kept his thoughts to himself for so long. They kept driving, and as the morning became afternoon, Gilbert talked about the painful self recriminations that had occupied his mind for more than a month. Ron listened quietly, watching the scenery and letting Gilbert shed the heavy burden of hopelessness. Ron had shouldered that burden before himself. More than once that day, he thought back to his service at the Da Nang Civil Hospital, South Vietnam. At one time he had been the only doctor for the pediatric section, where there were 60 beds and never less than 120 patients. Every night, the doctors had to leave the hospital for fear that the Viet Cong would come and kidnap them, meaning that the children would be left to the care of their parents. In the mornings, he would arrive at the hospital and begin the process of separating the dead from the dying. Coming to terms with so overwhelming a situation made it easier for him now to comfort Gilbert. In an intractable crisis, Dr. Case believed, one had to limit his energies to those duties he could perform and refrain from trying to understand.

"There are things you can do to help Terry," Ron said as they circled the city. "Think about what happens next. Where does Terry go when he leaves the hospital?"

Gilbert shrugged. "Dr. Cushman said something about a rehabilitation center, but Ron, he may not live through the day. He's back on the respirator. How can I think about anything else?"

"Whether he lives through the day, Gilbert, is something you have no control over."

Gilbert fought back his tears and Ron put his hand on his shoulder. "Terry's a fighter, Gilbert. A lot like his father. He'll make it."

Gilbert pulled the car over. He couldn't drive and cry at the same time. It was the thought of Terry being a lot like his father that opened the floodgates. Maybe if he hadn't been so much like his father he wouldn't have broken his spine.

* * *

Back in the hospital, Terry was growing angrier by the day. He understood the need to regain his independence from the respirator, but why so fast? Why were they making him fight so hard? He didn't know how many more times he could gather the resolve to overcome that constant desire to go to sleep and be done with it. Let go of life. He knew all he would have to do was accept that and he would die. But how could he quit when he hadn't even LIVED yet?

No matter how bad the respiratory checks were, when they were over, he begged the nurses to stay, not because he wanted to talk, just because he wanted somebody close by. He couldn't fall asleep unless someone else was in the room to make sure he didn't die in his sleep, with his guard down.

But they always wanted to talk, and he could only listen and pray for sleep or the strength to take a good, deep breath.

Terry was learning something about his own strength. With every battle to breathe, he became more familiar with that place inside of him where his strength resided. It was in that place that he felt God's presence now. Not out in the distant heaven he'd imagined all his life, but inside himself.

As the fights to breathe continued, Terry began devising strategies to keep his mind from noticing the sounds and the smells and the intensity of the pain. He lied to himself constantly. 'This doesn't hurt. This is not pain, it's just an experience I'm going through.'

He thought about riding horses a lot, especially when they turned on the suction to clear his lungs. He would close his eyes and see himself galloping bareback across the pasture behind his house in Portland. His head was low, close to Sheba's neck and his hair swept back by the wind. He could feel the rhythm of the horse's gait beneath him, and his senses were filled with the outdoors.

It was the only way Terry knew to keep his sanity.

* * *

April 2nd. It had been a week since Gilbert's ride with Ron Case and he was feeling somewhat better. He had been to the hospital library and checked out a book on spinal cord injuries, and a friend had given him a copy of the *Gymnastics Safety Handbook,* written by a former Olympic gymnastics coach and recommended by the National Secondary School Athletic Association.

He was reading the safety handbook that morning in the waiting room when Dr. Cushman walked in.

"Terry's coming along well," the doctor said. "The area around his injury has stabilized so we're going to take him off traction tomorrow. That means we'll remove the weight and take the screws out of his head

"That's great news," Gilbert said.

"What about his breathing?" Myrna asked.

"He's making progress," Cushman said. "Dr. Tizzard

thinks if his vital signs remain steady, we may be able to close the hole in his throat and let him start breathing on his own by the first of next week."

It was exactly what Gilbert had been hoping to hear. He couldn't control his excitement. "Have you told Terry yet?" he asked.

"No. If you like, you can tell him."

Gilbert and Myrna followed Dr. Cushman into the intermediate care room, and when the doctor had finished his examination and left, they stood over Terry's bed.

"We've got some good news," Gilbert said. "The doctors say your breathing is getting better and they'll be able to take you off the respirator next week."

Terry looked back with dull eyes. "I'm not ready," he whispered.

"Well, not now, but they seem to think you will be by next week."

Terry shook his head. "It's torture," he said. "It's like being under water."

"I know how tough it is," his father said, and Terry closed his eyes. "Everybody's praying for you. You can beat this thing."

"I'm GOING to beat it," Terry replied quietly.

The next morning, Myrna stayed with Terry through the respiratory check and thanked the nurses after they had connected the oxygen mask that would make breathing easier for him. She massaged his forehead and reassured him that he would be able to breathe on his own before very long.

"Maybe this will be the time I make it," he said with a smile, and Myrna nodded back.

The determination was evident in his eyes but 30 minutes later, it was obvious that Terry was having difficulty. There was a rasping sound to his breathing that had not been there before.

Myrna came to the bed and asked Terry if he was okay.

He nodded. "Fine," he whispered.

Terry knew something was wrong but he didn't know what. Throughout the rest of the day, he struggled against the rasping sound and fought to breathe. He didn't care how much it hurt, he was going to keep breathing until he couldn't breathe anymore. He wasn't asking for any help this time. Somehow, he made it through the night, but by the next morning, he had lost his strength. He had been off the respirator for 24 hours and his diaphragm had begun to hurt. This was a pain he hadn't experienced before. Like a pulled muscle. Then his diaphragm stopped working. He actually felt it stop on its own. "Air," he managed to say, barely loud enough for Myrna to hear.

She immediately ran into the hall, and soon the room was filled with activity. The nurses checked the oxygen flow, and made sure Terry's vital signs were holding steady.

"I need air," he whispered. His diaphragm was coming and going, like a fading battery. It would work for a moment, then stop again.

"Don't get excited, Terry," one of the nurses said. "That's why you can't get enough air. Just calm down."

As they were leaving the nurse patted Myrna's arm. "He'll be okay," she said. "He just needs to relax."

When the nurses had left the room, Terry closed his eyes. This was it. If they left him off the respirator now, he would die. He began to fade into unconsciousness, then caught himself. "No," he said. "I can't pass out now."

He concentrated on his diaphragm, struggling to keep it working. After 30 minutes, he convinced Myrna to call the nurse back in.

"What is it, Terry?" she said.

"You must hook me on right now or I will die," he whispered deliberately.

"Now, Terry. . . ."

He closed his eyes. "I can't get air."

The nurse looked at Myrna. "He really will be all right. He just has to fight through it." Then she smiled at Terry again. "Promise me you'll try to relax now. Dr. Tizzard will be here soon."

"Please call Mike," Terry said.

"Now, now, you're going to be okay. Just relax."

When the doctor finally arrived, Terry had been off the respirator for 28 hours and his face was blue. His oxygen level had dropped to 50 percent. Tizzard immediately ordered him back on the respirator. "Move fast!" he shouted.

Gilbert walked in as nurses hurried to set up the equipment. There must have been a dozen people in the room; all of them moving frantically. And in the middle of the room, Terry lay with his head fallen to the side. So still. So gray. He looked to Gilbert, like Christ lying at the foot of the cross.

Mike Parks had been off that day and when he found out what had happened, he was furious that he hadn't been called. "Let's make sure this thing is working right," he said. Terry was back on the respirator now, and Mike checked the oxygen mask Terry had been wearing. Then he examined the respirator cuff in Terry's windpipe. The cuff was inflatable and wrapped around the tube which let air from the respirator pass into Terry's lungs. When the cuff was inflated, it prevented the air from escaping back out.

"The cuff is deflated," Mike almost shouted. "No wonder you couldn't breathe."

Quickly, he removed the cuff and replaced it. When he was finished, he rested his hand on Terry's shoulder. "You were losing air everytime you took it in," he said, shaking his head. "Buddy, you put up one incredible fight. I don't know how you did it."

"Me either," Terry said.

"There's one good thing about it though," Mike said, smiling. "If you can make it through that, you can make it through anything."

* * *

On April 6th, the hole in Terry's throat was closed and the respirator removed from his room forever. The battle to breathe was not over, but the war to live seemed to be won.

Three days after they'd removed the respirator, Dr. Cushman returned to Terry's room for another of the regular examinations.

When the exam was over, Dr. Cushman stood by Terry's bed. "You're making excellent progress," he said. "The injury has stabilized and your respiratory function is getting better everyday. I know it's been hard, but you're almost through the worst of it."

He smiled at Terry.

"We're going to move you into regular care tomorrow," Cushman continued. "You'll be sitting up and riding around in a wheelchair before you know it."

"Almost through the worst of it. . . ." The words had sounded so good to him, but after Cushman left they lingered with the suspicious ring of false hope.

* * *

As Terry began to recover, a new battle began, in his mind.

Who was he? What was he? Was this a permanent condition? The fact that there were no answers made the questions all the more depressing. He wanted to know that he was still the same person. He wanted to feel like Terry Wilks again.

For a month he had asked the nurses to relax the rules against children in the serious care wards, so he could visit with David. They'd refused, and Terry became more and more depressed at not being able to see his little brother. He just wanted to SEE him.

Finally Gilbert came up with an idea.

From Terry's window, there was a view of the parking lot and a small park. Gilbert would take David out to the park so Terry could see him.

Terry watched them as they came into view, looking up at his window. Dad pointed at him and he could see David putting his hand over his eyes and squinting to see. For a split second he wanted to wave, then he caught himself. He couldn't wave so he couldn't think about it.

His Dad picked up David and held him up in the air, and David waved shyly. Terry started to cry. Would he ever be close to David again? Would he ever be close to anybody?

As spring came on, the view from his window became as depressing as the atmosphere in his room. Watching the dogwood and red bud trees bloom left him with a deep sense of self-pity. He couldn't look out the window without thinking about his legs. They were shrunken, shriveled, the size his arms had been before the accident. All of his fighting seemed so senseless to him when he saw how weak and frail he had become. His body made a mockery of the strength he depended on to fight the pain. He wanted to SEE that he was strong, but what he saw was irreversible weakness.

The fight was now raging inside Terry's head and everyday brought new challenges to his attitude from a hundred different directions. All of his feelings were new to him. His emotions were raw.

One Sunday afternoon, Tim Bullard and Jonetta Zerbee came down from Portland for a visit. The three of them talked and laughed for the first ten minutes they were there, like old times. It felt so good to laugh. Then Tim smiled oddly at Jonetta. "Terry, we've got a surprise for you," he said, "but we want to make sure it's okay with you if we bring it in."

"What is it?" Terry asked.

"It's our caps and gowns for graduation." Tim and Jonetta both looked at him expectantly.

"Yeah, sure, let's see 'em," Terry replied and Tim went into the hall, returning with a big box.

He opened the box and pulled out a long, shiny blue robe, holding it up for Terry to see. The sight of the robe caught Terry unprepared. He hadn't anticipated how beautiful it would look, so formal and distinctive, representing such a substantial achievement. This robe was meant to be worn by a healthy young man, not a weak, helpless kid, which was how he felt. Before he knew what to say, the tears had started running down his face.

"Oh, Terry, I was afraid this was a bad idea," Jonetta said and he could only shake his head. He'd begun to sob.

Jonetta was crying too now, leaning over Terry and hugging his shoulders, trying to comfort him. Tim was about to cry when he left the room.

"I'm so sorry," Jonetta said through her tears. "I'm so sorry."

* * *

But slowly, as he continued to grow stronger, Terry began to win the battle for his mind. No matter how hollow his victory over death seemed, the fact was; he was still alive. And he had found a strength within himself he didn't know he had.

Dr. Cushman suggested that Gilbert hire a private duty nurse to stay with Terry after he'd moved to orthopedics. By this time Gilbert and Myrna were both exhausted from the endless days and nights. They tried to always have one of them with Terry, and now with their failing energy, knew something had to be done.

By now, the walls of his room were covered with post cards and letters and a big bouquet of balloons was tied to the foot of the bed. Beside the bed, three grocery sacks were filled with letters from friends and well-wishers.

And Terry was starting to sit up. Once the tongs had been removed from his head, they'd begun raising him a little each day, letting his body readjust gradually after two months in the horizontal position. After a week, he took his first ride in a wheelchair, and felt another surge of hope. He wouldn't have to lie down for the rest of his life. He could move.

While Terry was growing stronger, Gilbert had begun investigating rehabilitation centers. Dr. Cushman had recommended several in the general area, but his first choice was the Spain Rehabilitation Center, located on the University of Alabama at Birmingham campus, in the heart of downtown Birmingham.

Gilbert, Myrna and Melvin, their corporate pilot,flew their single engine Beach Bonanza down and visited the center. The flight had been a bumpy one and the center looked just like another hospital, but they'd come away with a very good feeling about the place.

They saw people with injuries similar to Terry's—C-4's they called them because they'd been injured at the fourth vertebra level of their spinal cord. They saw one C-4 going down the hallway in his electric wheelchair, and another, a girl, smiling, happy, trying to get her arms to work. Anything seemed possible to Gilbert that day.

"Excuse me," he'd said to one nurse, "but have you ever seen a patient who was healed. I mean, who regained everything?"

"You mean have I ever seen a miracle?" she asked.

"Yes."

She looked him in the eye. "No," she said, leaving no doubt to her meaning.

Still, Gilbert's optimism was undiminished when he returned to Nashville and told Terry about the center. As he talked, describing the facilities and the patients, Terry began to imagine a resort, with dark-wooded cabins connected by walkways through beautifully manicured lawns, where the patients sat around the pool all day and played shuffleboard.

But for all of his Dad's excitement, Terry really didn't want to leave Memorial. He had made friends there. He had a routine that he could manage, and he was close to home, close to his friends.

* * *

It was a beautiful morning near the end of April, 1981, and Terry was looking forward to his first trip outside. His stay in Nashville was almost over. In a few days he would leave in an ambulance for Birmingham.

"Now remember," the nurse said as they rolled down the hall to the elevator. "We're not going very far so there's nothing to worry about. Just tell me if you have any problem."

They moved cautiously into the elevator and headed for the ground floor. The neck brace he was wearing now kept his head from falling to the side, and the chair back was slanted at a 45-degree angle.

When the elevator opened at the ground floor, Terry was suddenly conscious of his appearance. His chest was sunken and his skin pale. He imagined the people watching him as he rolled toward the exit, thinking how glad they were that they weren't like him.

But all thoughts of other people vanished when he finally got outside. It was a beautiful day, warm and vibrant with the smell of new growth.

Everything was so fresh. Terry looked around as the nurse pushed him into a grassy clearing. Every rock he hit jarred his body, sending waves of pain into his head. But when they finally stopped, Terry was able to relax and take in his surroundings. The trees seemed so green to him, now that he was out of the hospital. The warmth of the sun seemed to penetrate to his bones.

He had missed this more than he realized. Life was everywhere. For so long, Terry had been confined to the stale atmosphere of his hospital room. But now he felt different. He was still a part of this. He still had life in him.

"Lord, Please, Just My Hands!"

"Nobody will bother you," the woman said. The blue jeans and sneakers she wore only partially hid the fact that she was a nurse. "If a class comes in, just ignore them."

Terry stared at the ceiling when she left, praying that a class wouldn't come in. He was on a stretcher in an empty recreation room at Spain Rehabilitation Center, waiting while his parents met with the director of the center, Samuel L. Stover.

Terry shivered from the chill in the room. It certainly wasn't the resort he'd imagined—much more like a hospital except the nurses wore street clothes and they weren't as attentive as the nurses at Memorial had been. He'd noticed that, just in the hour since he'd arrived. They didn't seem to care as much about their patients. He was homesick.

'What will happen to me here?' he wondered again.

The word "rehabilitation" had been running through his mind for days. Did that mean regaining the use of his body or learning to live without it? He closed his eyes at the thought, fighting to stop the tears. He had to get SOMETHING back.

Whatever it took, he was willing to do it, but right now, all he could do was wait.

* * *

"Hello, Terry, I'm Libba."

He smiled at the pretty face looking down at him. She was in her early thirties with brown eyes and dark hair pulled back into a bun.

"We're going to work together on making you stronger," she said. "One of the first things we'll do is get you sitting up straighter in that wheelchair. But we'll do that gradually. I don't like my patients passing out on me."

"Good."

"Okay." She took a pencil out of her pocket and picked up her clipboard. "First we're going to take a little test. I want you to tell me when you feel anything. Do you feel anything now?"

Terry could not lean forward to see what she was touching. He only knew there was no feeling. Nothing.

"What about now?"

Nothing again.

The tests went on for thirty minutes. She asked him to raise his arms in front of him and to the side. She asked him to make a fist. By the time she was finished, Terry was disgusted. Angry. He couldn't do anything. How were they going to "rehabilitate" him when he couldn't pass the first test?

"Now we're going to do some range of motion exercises," Libba said. "I'm going to take you out of the chair."

Terry felt even more disgusted as she bent forward to pick him up, straddling his legs between hers, sliding her arms underneath his and locking her hands in back. He cringed as his face pressed into her neck. How could he be so helpless?

"There we go," she said as she positioned him in the middle of the mat. He hadn't realized how strong she was.

"All right, we start with the legs," she said, picking up his foot and slowly pushing his leg toward his chest. "You'll have to do your range of motion exercises everyday, Terry. Otherwise your tendons will tense up or shorten from lack of use. Even when you can't move, you have to get exercise."

Terry thought about his gymnastic workouts. He thought about running. Then his head fell to the side and he was staring at a set of parallel bars, two feet off the ground— as if God had placed it there to finish his train of thought. EVERYTHING about this place reminded him of what he could do before the accident. His physical ability had been one of his greatest sources of pride. He HAD to have it back.

He turned his concentration to the exercise, focusing his mind on Libba's movements, visualizing the muscles of his legs stretching and relaxing. Maybe if he believed the sensations hard enough, he would feel them.

* * *

The solarium at Spain was a big room on the third floor with a full view of dowtown Birmingham. Chairs were arranged around the walls and there were two pool tables at one end of the room. Terry was wheeled into the room by a pretty therapist named Cynthia, who would be leading that morning's group session.

Cynthia had come to Terry's room 30 minutes before, to introduce herself and tell him about group therapy.

"Everybody here has been through something that has changed their lives, but the fact is, Terry, there are no sick people here. You've all been released from hospitals and you all are getting ready to go back out into the world."

The therapy sessions, she explained, were helpful because everyone had a chance to talk about the problems of adjusting to the new reality.

"How do you like it here, Terry?" she'd asked him.

"Fine," he said quietly.

When she asked him how he liked the nurses, Terry didn't answer. Aside from his roommate who smoked incessantly and listened to his radio 24 hours a day, the thing he hated most about Spain was the nurses. They treated him like an object, not a person. He wanted to tell her about how roughly he'd been handled during his first slab bath. It wasn't humiliating enough to be dropped onto the stainless steel slab and watch yourself get hosed down like a car going through a carwash. The nurse had brought him back into his room and thrown him on the bed on his side. His arm had been pinned behind him and the nurse had turned around and pushed the wheelchair out of the room. "Nurse!" he'd yelled and she'd come back in. "My arm hurts."

"I was coming back," she said, pushing him over and jerking his arm from under his body.

Terry wanted to tell Cynthia about that incident, but he couldn't. It would only make the nurses treat him worse.

"You notice the nurses don't wear white?" she was saying. "That's because they aren't here to take care of you. They're here to help you learn how to live with a new set of rules. They're not going to do it for you, Terry. That's one of the most important things you will need to understand. You've got to do it for yourself."

When the group session finally began, Terry's mind wandered back to his conversation with Cynthia. "There are no sick people here," she'd said. Maybe he wasn't sick, but he certainly wasn't well either. Then what was he? The word appeared in his mind. "Handicapped." A wave of anger and fear washed over Terry.

He was NOT handicapped. He hated the word. Handicapped people weren't normal, but HE was normal. He was still Terry Wilks, no matter what had happened to his body.

* * *

Terry sat inside the metal A-frame with his arms resting in green canvas slings. Slowly, the weights were lowered and his arms raised to shoulder level, then back down. Up and down. He was starting to feel some strength coming back into his shoulders, but in his arms he still felt nothing.

The A-frame was in the occupational therapy room, where Terry went twice a day to "work on his motor skills." Across from the A-frame was a pair of wooden work benches, their orange paint tatooed with etchings left by exacto knives and woodworking tools. Separating the A-frame from the work benches was a shuffleboard court, painted on the floor. "There are a lot of people here who can use their hands," Terry thought, afraid to ask himself the question: "Will I be one of them before I leave?"

At least he liked the therapist. Linda was always in a good mood, happy to see him. When he was depressed she could bring him out of it.

"I can't do anything," Terry would say.

"Terry," she said, narrowing her eyes. "You can always do something."

She'd encouraged him to try typing. A mouthpiece was designed with a pencil-shaped piece of plastic sticking from it. She put it in Terry's mouth and he learned forward—the typewriter was sitting at almost a vertical angle. As he lowered his head, the stick began to shake. He tried to steady it, finally letting his head fall forward. The stick landed on the P. He pulled his head back and moved to hit the space bar, his chin almost touching his chest. Saliva was running down the stick and when he tried to swallow, the stick fell from his mouth. Terry labored to pull his head back to an upright position as a wave of dizziness came over him.

"That certainly is a handsome P," Linda said as she tilted his chair back to a 45-degree angle.

Terry closed his eyes. His neck was so weak he couldn't type more than one letter, but what was the point of it? He was supposed to be learning how to use his hands, not his neck.

* * *

On Friday morning, Dr. Stover came in to visit Terry with a group of other doctors, members of the staff. Stover held up the X-ray of Terry's spine and talked about his rate of recovery. The vertebrae were almost stable now, as was the scar tissue on the spinal cord. They talked about his diet— they'd eliminated all calcium and were making him drink ten glasses of water a day—and they talked about his bladder and bowel training.

Terry listened patiently, waiting for them to get to the subject of his physical rehabilitation. He wanted to hear what Stover had to say about his regaining the use of his hands.

"Any questions?" Stover said when he'd finished, and before Terry had time to think, they were saying good-bye to him and leaving the room.

* * *

From the first, there had been no question that Gilbert and Myrna would move to Birmingham for the duration of Terry's stay at Spain. Gilbert found a nice, three bedroom house to rent on a hill overlooking the city, and Myrna was finally able to take care of David again. Diane was still in school, but she would come down after graduation.

Things in general had been looking up for Gilbert and Myrna since they'd arrived in Birmingham and had a chance to rest for a week or so. The ordeal in Nashville had exhausted them more than they'd realized.

News was good from Wilks Publications as well. Sales figures in the new markets were up. Not much, but enough to suggest a trend. If it kept up, the company would be making money again by the end of May. It was very gratifying to Gilbert that his company had survived two months without him. He had built something stronger than he'd realized.

And now Terry seemed to be progressing so well. He had such a good attitude, the therapist had told him, and everyday he was getting better—coming back stronger than ever.

As soon as they had moved into the house, Gilbert asked Dr. Stover if Terry could visit them. Stover thought it was a good idea. He agreed to allow Terry out of the center for a day, as soon as he was strong enough to go without the neckbrace.

It was a beautiful spring morning and Gilbert was excited as he drove the station wagon down the winding road from their house to the center. Terry's first trip away from the hospital setting since his accident was going to be a big day.

Gilbert had pushed Terry out to the car himself, talking happily about the fun they were going to have when they got home. Myrna had baked a beautiful cake. When they got to the car, Gilbert opened the passenger door to the front seat.

He'd thought about laying Terry in back, but the idea had seemed degrading, as if he were treating his son like a piece of luggage. Gilbert wanted Terry to feel NORMAL today.

When he had to lift Terry out of the chair and put him on the seat, Gilbert began to feel panic. What if he dropped him? It wasn't going to be easy. He locked his hands behind Terry and strained to pull him out of the chair, losing his balance and having to drop him back in the chair for fear of falling over backwards.

Finally, he succeeded in getting him into the car and only then did he realize that there was only a seat belt and no shoulder harness. He hadn't thought about the fact that Terry couldn't sit up straight by himself. But that was okay, Gilbert thought. He could hold Terry with his hand.

The drive up to the house had been torturous. Terry was frightened by every car on the road, every stoplight, every turn. Gilbert kept his hand on Terry's chest, but twice he fell forward at stops. By the time they got to the house, they were both exhausted; trying to realize what was really happening.

It was a delicious lunch. Myrna had fixed all of Terry's favorite things and he'd enjoyed the meal, but other things seemed to be on his mind. He'd asked David to come and talk to him after lunch, but David was afraid of the wheelchair. Finally, Terry had gone outside to look at the view of Birmingham.

Sitting alone, Terry thought about his hands. Being with his family was nice, but it could not remove the heaviness he felt when he thought about his hands, and he could not stop thinking about them.

He wanted to be able to hold somebody again; write; paint; play the guitar; brush his teeth; scratch his ear; tie his shoe lace; comb his hair; shave; fasten a button; wave good-bye. He couldn't make his mind stop. Everything there was TO DO seemed tied to the use of hands. How could he go on living without them?

Tears started rolling down his cheeks and he wanted more than anything to stop. He couldn't stand to let his family see him cry. He hated feeling sorry for himself. He just wanted to know something, one way or the other. Was he going to get his hands back or wasn't he? That's all he wanted to know.

* * *

The tension continued to mount inside Terry with each passing day. He worked hard in therapy and was encouraged by his progress, but he was still in the dark about his condition. Finally on his second Friday at the center, he decided the time had come.

When the doctors entered his room for the weekly rounds,

Terry already knew what he was going to say. He waited as Dr. Stover proceeded with his assessment of Terry's condition. Then, when the men were filing out of the room, Terry called out to Dr. Stover and asked him to remain behind for a moment.

Dr. Stover smiled slightly. Like Dr. Cushman in Nashville, Dr. Stover rarely showed emotion.

"I want to ask you a question," Terry said, struggling, for no physical reason, to catch his breath. "I want to know if I'll ever be able to use my hands?"

Dr. Stover cleared his throat. "Terry, never say never, but to be honest with you, it's unlikely you will regain the use of any of your body below the shoulder. There have been cases. . . ."

The rest of what he said played on like background music. Terry nodded and responded but he wasn't listening.

He'd known it from the first day he was here; the first time Linda had him type with his mouth; the first time Libba pricked him with a pin. Now he couldn't escape the truth of it. All of the dreams were gone. The tears began to flow from Terry's eyes again and this time he couldn't stop them.

It meant he was a quad, like every other C-4 he'd met since he'd been here. Why had he thought he was any different? He didn't know why, but he had. Visions began flashing through his mind of all the things he couldn't do. 'No, God,' he cried, 'don't let me think about that'. But he couldn't turn it off, and the more he thought about it the more he cried.

The trauma of realizing he was paralyzed had been hard to live through, but realizing he wouldn't have his hands was just as bad. The difference between a paraplegic and a quad was the same as that between a para and someone who could walk. He'd lost everything.

Finally the tears stopped and Terry longed for a handkerchief so he could blow his nose and wipe his face. The

pillow was wet against his neck. The thought of blowing his
nose made the tears come again. It was no longer a joke for
him. Now blowing his nose was a physical necessity just like
the urine catheter and the laxatives. He couldn't let any of his
pipes get clogged. That's all his body was, a collection of pipes
and machinery that had to be kept working so his brain could
live.

"No!" Terry cried in disgust. He couldn't stand the thought.
He wasn't just a brain. Maybe he couldn't move certain parts,
but the parts were there. He was still Terry Wilks.

He sniffed as hard as he could, barely drawing in a strong
breath, aching for the ability to wipe the sticky dampness from
his face. That was it, no more crying. If he couldn't wipe away
his tears, he WOULDN'T cry. Terry didn't think about
anything but his face, loathing the way it felt, blaming his tears
for reminding him of all the things he couldn't do.

When the tears had stopped, Terry opened his eyes and
stared at the ceiling, blinking until he could see clearly. He was
alive. That was a fact. He still had a family and friends who
loved him. He could type. Maybe he could even paint again.
People painted with their mouths. He braced himself, quieting
the self-pity inside of him before it had a chance to grow.

He thought about his graduation and the friends he hadn't
seen since he'd come to Birmingham. He wanted to be with
them again, to let them see that he was still Terry, still their
friend. He hadn't given up just because of the accident. The
vision of himself on the stage, accepting his diploma flashed in
his mind. He wouldn't even be able to hold out his hand to
accept it. But that wasn't the point. He wanted to prove that
he could do it.

* * *

Gilbert and Myrna were preparing to leave for Spain that
afternoon when Dr. Stover's office called. The doctor wanted

them to stop by and see him before they saw Terry.

When they got to his office, Stover invited them in and they sat at his small conference table.

"Terry stopped me after rounds today and asked if he'd ever be able to use his hands again," he said.

Gilbert and Myrna were suddenly still, their eyes riveted on Stover's face. "I told him it was unlikely. I think it's time Terry knew that he will probably be this way the rest of his life."

Myrna looked down at her own hands. How could it be true? After all the time and all the hope and prayers for recovery, their worst unspoken fears had come true. Terry was paralyzed from the neck down. He couldn't use his arms or legs. How was that fair? How could she ever think anything was fair again?

* * *

When Gilbert and Myrna walked into Terry's room, it was obvious to him that they'd been crying. They smiled and tried their best to show him they could still be strong.

"We talked to Dr. Stover," Gilbert managed to say, catching himself as his voice broke.

"It's okay," Terry said. He had stopped crying several hours ago and the memory of his tears still brought on his anger. "Don't worry about it. It's going to be okay."

Myrna blinked back the tears as she hugged him. Was he trying to make them feel better? She looked at his face for some sign of the pain he was trying to hide, but his face appeared calm. Drained, but calm.

"It's okay, Mom," he said and to her, he suddenly sounded older—even older than she.

"Hey, Dad," Terry said. "Can I ask you a question?"

Gilbert stepped closer to the bed.

"Remember when you told me that you were going to ask Dr. Stover about going to graduation?"

"Yes," Gilbert said.

"Well, I'd like to do that. I'd like to go home for graduation."

"Oh, Terry, I don't think. . . ."

"Ask him, Dad. Please."

* * *

Dr. Stover said no. Terry wasn't strong enough yet. If anything happened while he was gone, Spain would be liable. It wasn't up to him, it was up to the insurance company.

Terry begged and pleaded. He was strong enough to go to the apartment. They'd only have to be gone for two days. At the rate he was going, in a week's time, he'd be strong enough to sit up straight in the wheelchair all the time.

Finally Stover agreed to reserve final judgment until closer to the day of departure. He wanted to see if Terry would continue to progress.

* * *

It was the Monday before graduation. Terry had five days to prove to Dr. Stover that he was strong enough to go home for a weekend. That morning, he told Linda in occupational therapy he'd decided to start painting. She delightedly set up the easel and prepared the paints and brush. His first painting, he declared, would be a sailboat.

* * *

The afternoon group session had been very interesting as well, and now he was in physical therapy, ready to get a workout.

Terry closed his eyes as Libba pulled him out of his chair and set him down on the mat. He had only recently noticed how good she smelled. He had noticed a lot of things about Libba lately and suddenly he realized, for the first time since his accident, he felt attracted to someone of the opposite sex.

"So what did ya'll talk about in group?" Libba said as she

began his first range of motion exercise.

"Sex," he replied.

"Oh, that sounds like fun," she said.

"There was a C-2 who led the discussion and he was really a cool guy. He seemed happy about life."

"Now that's an accomplishment," Libba replied. "C-2's usually don't live. Their breathing stops before they can get emergency help. They REALLY have to fight."

Terry nodded, thinking about his own fight. It was hard to imagine that anyone could fight harder than that. "Anyway, he said he didn't have any problem with girls at all. He gets turned on just like everybody else."

"Of course," Libba replied as she pushed Terry's left leg up to his chest.

"He said he doesn't care about having a family or anything permanent with a girl. He's just satisfied with talking to them and flirting with them and maybe a little more. . . ." He smiled and she smiled back.

"How do you feel about that, Terry?" she asked. "About having a family?"

He shrugged. "I don't know, I always wanted a family."

"Did you talk about that?"

He shook his head. In fact, the therapist had talked about the possibility of having children. She said men had the ability to have an erection, but not to ejaculate, because that signal came from the brain. There were instances of semen being removed by surgical means, but the therapist knew very little about that.

"Women are lucky," she'd said. "All of the female reproductive parts keep working. A paralyzed woman can give birth."

But Terry's thoughts were now on his own future, and he remembered something else she'd said:

"You have a sexuality. As long as you're a male or a female you have a sexuality and you should never be ashamed of it.

Experience it. It's an important part of your life."

As Libba continued exercising him, their conversation turned to other topics. They talked about her children and about his plans for graduation. They were already making arrangements, even though Dr. Stover had not given his final approval.

"Oh, I heard about your painting," Libba said. "I can't wait to see it."

"It may take a year," he laughed. "Every stroke takes ten minutes. But I'll finish it one of these days."

"We'll just have to work on making your neck stronger," Libba said. "I don't think we've ever had a patient who learned how to paint while they were here."

Terry smiled. "When I finish the sailboat, I'll paint something for you."

"I'd like that," Libba said.

When she leaned over to pick him up, Terry felt different. He no longer felt like her patient. 'I'm going to kiss her,' he thought. Suddenly his heart was pounding. She smiled at him as he started to lean forward. 'No, don't do it,' he said to himself. 'This lady's married. To a doctor. She's got two kids. Everybody in the place is going to be watching. This is crazy.'

"Terry," she said with a soft laugh in her voice. "What are you doing?"

He grinned back at her. "Oh, nothing," he said. The moment was gone and he shoved it away from embarrassment.

But back in his room that afternoon, he couldn't get his mind off it. There had been a chemistry between them, a spark like he'd always felt when he was attracted to a girl. And she seemed to have felt it too. Even without his body, he could still feel that spark inside. Having the ability to create that spark was what he called having a sexuality. And feeling it now made him feel more alive, more human, than he had in weeks.

* * *

Dr. Stover finally decided to let Terry go home during rounds Friday morning. He had shown improvement in all areas of his treatment. He'd earned the trip. But there were a whole list of things he needed to remember. This wasn't going to be a pleasure trip, by any means. A small relapse and he could be back in the hospital attached to a respirator.

Gilbert spent half an hour with the doctor, writing down all of the precautions they would need to take. Terry could leave that afternoon, but he would have to be back at the center in 48 hours.

When Stover left, Terry felt his spirits soar. He'd taken the first step. The morning became mass confusion as Gilbert and Myrna hurried to pack everything and prepared to leave. Terry loved the excitement and he was feeling very good when Cynthia came by. She wanted to congratulate him and wish him a good trip.

"I just want you to know, Terry, that it's going to feel strange, being around all your old friends again. But remember one thing: you can be a teacher. You've been through something they can't even imagine. You're special because of that, and you can pass it on."

* * *

At 3 p.m. on Friday, May 14, the Wilks family station wagon pulled away from Spain Rehabilitation Center. In the back, Terry was lying on an orthopedic stretcher, staring at the ceiling fifteen inches above his head. His wheelchair was strapped on top of the car.

They would miss the consecration service that evening, but Mr. Brewer had agreed to reschedule Terry's part of the service—answering the challenge for the senior class—for Saturday morning. Then there was the senior party that night in the gym and graduation exercises Sunday morning.

Terry asked his mother to check him on his speech again. His Mom had written it down for him one night while they were still waiting for Dr. Stover to make his decision. Terry particularly liked the ending of the speech:

"So now, with Joshua as he stood over the banks of the River Jordan, I will say that as for me and my class, we will serve the Lord."

The ending was dramatic, he thought, especially if he paused before saying, *"we will serve the Lord."*

As they drove north, Terry imagined giving the speech as he would have given it before the accident. He envisioned himself standing in front of the church, gesturing, speaking forcefully as he looked around at the congregation.

He couldn't think about that. The speech he would give tomorrow would be just as strong, just as forceful. Maybe he couldn't gesture, or have eye contact with his audience, but the speech would be just as good. He had to show everyone that he could do exactly what he would have done had he not been injured.

He imagined the grand reception he would receive when all his friends saw him. He thought about the three grocery sacks filled with letters from his friends, and his chest began to swell in anticipation. He was going home!

* * *

There was a real sense of triumph for Gilbert and Myrna as they drove along Highway 109 from Portland to the Highland community. So many prayers had been answered. But they couldn't help being apprehensive about the shock of their friends when they would see how truly helpless Terry was.

It was still light as they turned into the Highland Academy

campus, past the Highland Church and down the hill to Old Fountain Head Road, then left past the gym.

They drove up the steep driveway and into the back yard so they could bring Terry in through the kitchen door, and not try to carry him up the front steps. When they opened the door, a large banner welcomed them, hanging across the length of the dining room.

"Look, Terry," Gilbert said. "Can you see it? It says 'Welcome Home Terry.' It must be twenty feet long."

"Wow," Terry said. "That's great!"

They had a quick dinner and then Gilbert began preparing Terry for bed. It was an odd feeling for Terry that night. It looked so much like home, but it didn't feel like home.

* * *

Low clouds had blown in and blocked the sun that morning as they drove to church. It had been a frantic morning. A group of Terry's friends had come over and joked around until Gilbert finally had to shoo them out so he could get Terry ready. They'd dressed him in his cap and gown, then placed him in the back of the station wagon for the drive to church.

When they arrived, Pastor Ricks was out front waiting for them. He helped Gilbert take Terry out of the car and put him in the wheelchair.

After Gilbert made sure Terry was straight in the chair and his leg bag was concealed beneath his pants, they started into the church. The other students in Terry's class had already formed the line leading inside, but when they saw Terry come into the foyer, the line broke apart. Robbie, Rosalie, Jonetta, Tim, Pat, Lori, Gerald—everyone gathered around him. They wanted to hug him, touch him. But there wasn't time. Pastor Ricks urged them back in line so the ceremony could begin.

Once Terry had found his place in line, Gilbert and Myrna

hurried into the sanctuary and took seats near the back. All of the rushed activity to get Terry home for graduation was over. They'd made it. As Gilbert looked around the congregation and saw the friendly faces smiling back at him, waving hello, he had to catch himself. The tears were starting to come. So many people had prayed so hard for this moment. It was such an incredible victory. And yet, it was a defeat as well. Terry was paralyzed. He couldn't walk down the aisle. Gilbert could no longer check the flow of his tears.

The music started and slowly the students began to file in toward the front of the church. A short, wooden ramp had been constructed so that Terry's wheelchair could make it onto the platform with the other students.

As each student entered the sanctuary, the electricity seemed to grow. Every person was turned around in their seat, waiting. The only sound was the quiet playing of the organ. And then Terry appeared at the door. As if by instinct, the entire congregation rose to its feet and stood in rapt silence as the young man in the wheelchair was pushed onto the stage. The only sounds were the clicking of the wheels and the sniffs of those in the audience trying to control their emotions.

On stage, a different kind of tension gripped Terry. He was about to deliver his speech. He couldn't think about the dizziness he felt, or the sensation that he was about to slip out of the chair because his gown was so slick. He couldn't listen to Elder Watson's opening message or look around the congregation at his friends. He could only think about his speech.

And then, he heard himself introduced. His chair was at a 45-degree angle, so he could not see everything, but he could see Jonetta stand up and approach him with the microphone. She smiled at him and Terry nodded, clearing his throat.

"Elder Watson," he said, "as pastor of our class it is my

privilege to represent the seniors of 1981 in responding to your message."

He looked straight ahead at the balcony, speaking slowly. His voice was loud and clear over the public address system as he spoke of the qualities necessary to achieve God's purpose and plan for our lives—self-denial, caring, and dependence upon God. As he came to the end of the speech, his confidence was strong. He was going to make it.

"So now, with Joshua as he stood over the banks of the River Jordan, I will say that as for me and my class, we will serve the Lord."

He'd made it!

* * *

When the service was over, Terry couldn't wait to get outside and see his friends. His moment of triumph had finally arrived. With Ricky pushing the chair, he made his way into the church parking lot. A small group of his friends immediately surrounded him and he felt a wave of warmth wash over him. This was what he had wanted. As Terry fell into conversation with Jonetta, the others drifted away, but not too far. Then Tim came over, then Robbie and Rosalie. His friends all wanted to talk to him.

But as Terry talked, he noticed other friends standing off at a distance. When their eyes would meet, they would smile and wave, but they seemed afraid to approach him. "How you doin'?" he would yell, and they would smile back. "Great, Terry, how are you?"

"I'm fine," he would reply.

And then his Dad told him it was time to head home.

"See you tonight at the gym," Terry yelled to Tim as he was placed in the seat of the station wagon. The senior class party was that night and Terry didn't plan to miss it, even though he hadn't been in the gym since his accident. He wasn't going to think about that though. He was home for graduation, not to confront bad memories.

But there was a nagging vision that stuck in his mind as he rode home. It was the look on the faces of his friends who stayed away from him after the service. Suddenly, the love and affection of his closest friends didn't matter. All he could think about were the friends who'd kept their distance. What did they see when they looked at him? A freak?

At home that afternoon, a steady stream of visitors kept Terry's mind off his other thoughts. Joanne and her family came by for lunch, and Terry seemed to truly enjoy himself as Joanne fed him. But there was an underlying current of confusion. Ever since the accident, Joanne had been different. She wanted to be with him all the time and when they were together, she always seemed to be touching him, stroking his hair, kissing his cheek. Terry didn't understand the change in her. Was all this attention just because she felt sorry for him? He didn't know, but he wasn't going to ask her to stop it. Not now. He needed it too much.

As hard as Gilbert tried, he couldn't make Terry rest that afternoon. There was too much excitement. When Joanne's family had finally left, Gilbert pushed Terry back to Diane's old room for a nap, only to hear the doorbell ring. It was Jonetta and her older sister, Johanna, and Terry insisted on seeing them. Gilbert couldn't say no, especially when he remembered the way Terry's eyes had lit up when she'd visited him in the hospital. His eyes had lit up that same way now, as she walked into the room with her radiant smile.

That night, Gilbert strongly suggested that Terry stay home. He'd had too much activity. Who knew what might happen if he kept pushing himself so hard? Think about what Dr. Stover had said. Nobody would mind if he stayed home. Everybody would understand.

"Dad, I'm a senior and this is senior class night. I'm going."

By the time Terry got to the gym that night, he had thoroughly prepared himself for the shock of returning to the scene of his accident. He wasn't going to think about it. When he looked at the spot where he'd fallen, he wasn't going to remember anything. He was only going to think about his friends and the occasion that brought him back to this place.

More than anything else, he did not want to cry.

A stage had been erected at one end of the gym and as soon as Terry was ready, the class filed onto the stage so the program could begin. Several people sang songs. One girl sang a song she'd written about Terry and when she finished there was a standing ovation.

Then they began showing childhood pictures of the various members of the class. As each picture was displayed, there were catcalls and jokes from the others in the class and gradually Terry began to laugh too. Gina Sims, a black girl who had always seemed distant toward Terry, now was leaning over and joking with him at each picture. She wasn't self conscious at all and her laughter was like a tonic for Terry. "Look at Tim," she said. "Boy, he looked funny."

Terry laughed, feeling like part of the gang again. Then his pictured appeared on the screen, two years old, wearing swimming trunks, laughing at the camera with his hands outstretched. When the picture appeared, an awkward silence suddenly fell over the students. There were no jokes, no catcalls.

"Now there's a real stud," Terry said suddenly, and the tension was broken. Gina burst out laughing.

"You call that a stud?" she said, and Terry grinned happily at her.

"You better believe it."

By the time they said goodnight to everyone and finally got home it was one a.m. He had to be ready for the graduation ceremony at ten the next morning. Everyone was exhausted.

* * *

The graduation ceremony was held in the gym Sunday morning. Pastor Ricks had asked Gilbert if he would lead the opening prayer before the ceremony began, and he'd gladly accepted. Now, as he sat on the stage waiting for the students to enter, Gilbert was filled with emotion. So much had happened. The pain they had lived through these last 90 days had so overwhelmed him that he could not fully enjoy this moment. His heart seemed torn between happiness and sadness.

Then the music began and the first students entered the gym. They walked single file down the center aisle and up the ramp onto the stage. Gilbert could see the pride in their eyes, realizing the personal sense of accomplishment each of them felt. Then Terry entered the gym and a sudden, thunderous ovation began.

It was so loud that it startled Gilbert. As Terry rolled up the ramp onto the stage, the applause continued. As he was situated at the end of the row of chairs, it grew louder. And it continued. Gilbert looked into the faces of those in the audience, and seeing their tears, he could not hold back his own. The room seemed to be lifted up from the outpouring of love for his son.

Finally the applause stopped. Everyone was seated and Principal Brewer began the ceremony. He talked about the unique character of the Class of '81. He talked about Terry, whose courage and faith was an inspiration, not only to his classmates, but to everyone.

Then it was time to award the diplomas. As his turn approached, Terry began to imagine his introduction. "... religious vice president of the student association; winner of the best all-around male gymnast trophy; pastor of his class; most likely to succeed. . . ."

Finally it was his turn.

"Terry Wilks," Mr. Brewer said in his strong clear voice, "Class pastor."

The applause began again, not as loud this time, nor as moving. Ricky pushed him forward and Mr. Brewer placed the diploma in Terry's lap. He smiled and nodded and Ricky pushed him back to his place. Somehow, despite the overwhelming outpouring of affection, despite everything, he felt disappointed.

* * *

There were lots of people to say good-bye to when the ceremony was over.

"Yeah, I have to go back down to Birmingham for another month," he told Tim and Rosalie. "But I'll be back this summer."

"We'll see you then," Tim said.

Then his father was standing beside him. "We'd better get going. We've got to be back by five."

They paused to take some pictures, then Terry was loaded into the back of the car, along with his diploma and the presents he'd received, and the Wilkses pulled away from the gym.

They drove back to the house briefly to pick up some things, but Terry was ready to leave. Something had changed. Even with his closest friends, Terry felt like a stranger. He thought about the faces of his friends who had stayed away, and his introduction when he received his diploma. Why had they left out all of his achievements? It was as if they'd said, 'We don't recognize these qualities in you anymore.'

He felt like he'd been wearing a mask of the old Terry Wilks all weekend, but behind that mask was someone else. It wasn't his friends who had changed. He had changed. He was a different person now, with a new life and a new attitude.

"I'm only three months old," Terry thought to himself, and suddenly, the truth of the statement hit him. He WAS a new person.

College,
Girls and
Fun Times

From the window of their kitchen, Myrna looked out across the lawn to the split rail fence that separated the backyard from the pasture. Terry was sitting in his wheelchair near the fence, and his horse, Goldie, was grazing just on the other side. It was a sight Myrna had gotten used to in the weeks since Terry had come home, but one that still evoked a deep sadness. Soon they would have to sell Goldie.

For Terry, sitting back by the fence had become a daily ritual. It seemed like he'd never spent much time thinking before the accident—always on the go, hurrying from one thing to the next. And now that he had all the time in the world to think, it was the one thing he didn't want to do, because his thoughts were too painful.

His first week back home, Terry vowed to himself to keep his spirits up, but even in that short time, the limits of his new life became painfully clear. He hadn't realized just how active he'd been before his accident.

As his mind wandered, Goldie came to the fence and looked over at him.

"You need a good grooming," Terry said, looking into her big brown eyes. "You need some exercise too. You're getting fat."

Terry thought about his own weight. He'd lost 50 pounds since the accident, but finally he was beginning to gain it back. Being able to eat his mother's cooking again was one of the things he enjoyed most about being home. But it wasn't enough. His arms and legs were half the size they'd been before. His stomach sagged out like a beer belly because he had no control over the muscles that held it in. Thinking about his body made him feel like a wimp. He couldn't do anything. His entire life— his existence—was suddenly subject to the presence of other people. He was TOTALLY DEPENDENT.

What could he do by himself? Watch TV? Sure, that was one thing he could manage, as long as he didn't have to change channels. He couldn't read a book unless someone was there to turn the pages. He couldn't take a ride in his car unless someone else was driving. He couldn't ride his horse.

Whatever he did required asking for help and he hated that more than anything. It seemed like the only time he ever spoke to anyone anymore was to ask them to do something for him. If he needed a drink of water, someone had to put a straw in it and hold it up so he could drink.

The dependence, more than anything else, depressed him. It was exactly the opposite of the way he'd been before the accident. He hardly ever asked for help; he offered it. Unselfishness had been such a cornerstone of his self image, that his dependence on others was all the more offensive to him. He could not afford to think that way anymore. He had to reprogram his mind.

At least he could paint. It wasn't very entertaining, but it kept him busy. Mostly it was hard work. It had taken him two weeks to finish the sailboat he painted for Linda back at Spain, and he'd been working on a kitten for almost six weeks now, which he planned to give to Joanne when he finished it. Trying to hold his head steady enough to control the brush was still the most difficult part of the process. His neck was getting stronger, but he still had a long way to go. At least painting was easier than drawing, because the brush was so much more forgiving than a pencil or pen.

Certain things had been hard for him, however. For one thing, Libba had changed. After he returned from graduation, she'd let him know that it was time for some heavy exercise. Physical therapy became strictly business.

After Libba, Terry had made another friend on the staff. Her name was Wendy and she was a student nurse. She began visiting Terry not long after he returned from graduation and they hit it off almost immediately. She was only a couple of years older than Terry and truly seemed to enjoy the time she spent reading to him, holding the newspaper, turning the pages and joking with him about the things they would read. They'd gone out on a date together. She'd invited him to church with her one Sunday night. After a lot of encouragement from his Dad, he decided to go.

The church service had been quiet and reserved and afterwards, they'd gone to a local restaurant and Terry and Wendy had talked until it closed.

Terry felt the same chemistry with Wendy he'd felt with Libba. But as the days went by, he saw her attention drawn to others, just as Libba's had been. A new boy came on the ward, injured in a motorcycle accident that had disabled his brain as well as his body. Terry could see Wendy's attention being drawn to the other patient. He felt frustrated, knowing there was nothing he could do to make her come back to him. Would he ever have a girl friend again? He didn't know, but one thing seemed clear—he couldn't make them stay. If girls stayed with him from now on, it would be because they chose to.

* * *

Terry's spirits rose again the day his Dad arrived with the new van. Gilbert had spent a lot of his time in Birmingham researching the various needs of quadriplegics, and transportation was one of the biggest. Terry couldn't be expected to ride around in the back of the station wagon. He needed a van with an hydraulic lift for his wheelchair and wheel wells to anchor the chair in place once inside.

The van Gilbert found was perfect. It was shiny, metallic gray with royal blue highlights on the outside, and decorated with carpet and paneling on the inside. It had been owned by a woman whose husband was wheelchair bound, so it was equipped with everything Terry would need. And it looked good. That's what Terry liked.

How well Terry remembered the day his Dad first brought the van for him to see. He remembered how it gleamed in the sun as his chair was pushed onto the hydraulic lift. Once inside the van, he loved being able to sit up and look out at the scenery. Maybe he was paralyzed, but at least he was going to ride in style.

Terry didn't have the same feeling, however, when Gilbert came to his room one afternoon with his new wheelchair. More than the van, more than anything in Terry's life, the wheelchair would become his constant companion. Libba had spent hours on the telephone, trying to find the best chair available for the quadriplegic. The critical factor for Terry would be the controls. As she made her calls, Libba discovered that a new control system had just been developed. The new control was called a "sip and puff" mechanism. A straw-like plastic tube, attached to the back of the chair, was bent around in front of the driver's face like the microphone on a pilot's headset, and he controlled the chair by sipping and blowing into the plastic tube.

The day the chair arrived at the hospital with the new "sip and puff" attachment, everyone was hoping to see the same

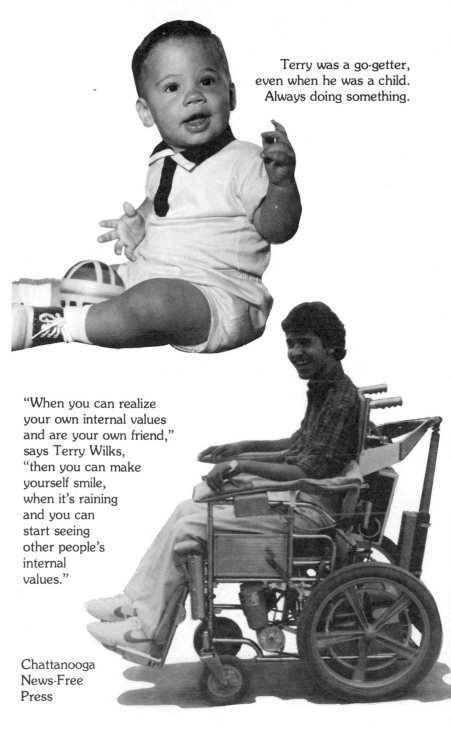

Terry was a go-getter,
even when he was a child.
Always doing something.

"When you can realize
your own internal values
and are your own friend,"
says Terry Wilks,
"then you can make
yourself smile,
when it's raining
and you can
start seeing
other people's
internal
values."

Chattanooga
News-Free
Press

7—T.

Terry, Diane and "Princess" ready for a joy ride."

Terry laughing at Diane, the "Baby" of the family.

Summer, 1984, three years after becoming paralyzed, Diane and Terry are still close.

Terry's little
brother, David.

THE WILKS FAMILY-Spring, 1984:
Gilbert, Terry, David, Diana, and Myrna

Dr. Stover gave Terry
a 48-hour leave to go
to graduation.

Terry and Gymnist
Coach, Dan Herzberg

Terry with classmates,
Lori Wicks and Rosalie Parrish

Jonetta talks with Terry
at graduation.

SPAIN REHABILITATION CENTER: Terry's first date after his accident was Wendy, one of the student nurses.

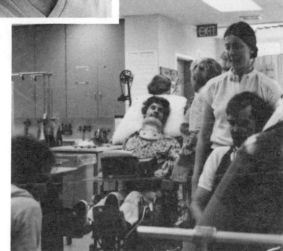

Terry, wearing a neck brace. Libba, physical therapist, who became a close friend of Terry's, helps another patient.

Terry and friend, Larissa, who was paralyzed in a driving accident.

Terry, age 18, six months before the accident.

At the White House

Joanne and Terry

At the beach

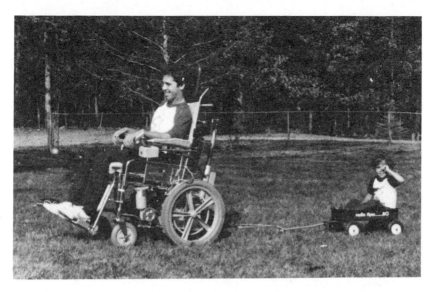

Terry and his brother, David, having fun in the back yard.

David, Terry and Diane

SCHOOL DAYS
Lori Wicks,
Terry Wilks,
Voted Most Courteous

Rosalie Parrish,
Terry Wilks,
Voted Most Likely
To Succeed.

HIGHLAND ACADEMY
Gymnastics Team

Terry

Best All-Around
1979-80 School Year

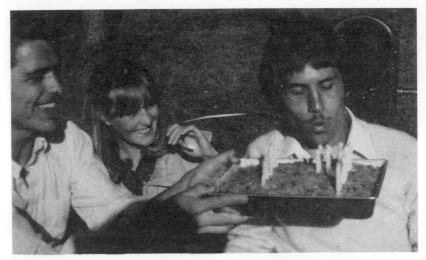

Terry blows all 19 candles out as Eddie and Audrey look on.

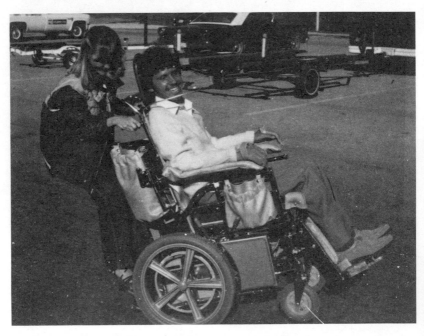

"Come on, Audrey, jump on the back and
let's see if we can pop a wheelie!"

Being casual,
age 21,
three years
after becoming
paralyzed.

Terry with friend, Susan.

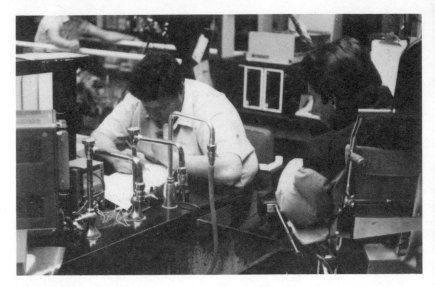

Dr. Petrofsky invited Terry to sit with him
and discuss his research.

Terry and Nan Davis hit it off right away. She was a
part of Dr. Petrofsky's research project and she was
excited about seeing herself on 60-Minutes.

Dr. Ron Case, family doctor and personal friend

"Thanks to the expertise and moral support of my doctors, I am alive today!"
—Terry

Dr. Arthur Cushman, neurosurgeon, Nashville.

Dr. Samuel Stover, Spain Rehabilitation Center, Birmingham.

Dr. Barth Green, right, neurosurgeon and researcher, University of Miami, hopes to cure paralysis soon. Marc Buoniconti, center paralyzed in a football accident, and his father, ex-Miami Dolphins football great, Nick Bounicanti, have helped establish the "Miami Project to Cure Paralysis" Fund, 1600 NW 10th Ave., Miami, FL 33136.

Mauri

Terry, Ken and
Joni Earickson Tada
at Abilities Unlimited
Convention, Anaheim,
California.

Terry's First Colored Painting.
It was Joni's paintings
that encouraged Terry
to paint by mouth.

About My Paintings: A dear friend posed as the subject for a composition featuring herself handling a horse, and is affectionately entitled, "Mauri." A more simplistic design revealing spirit and freedom was a natural, thus the single horse "Firefly." The rose, "With Love," is a favorite piece of mine. It is gold and silver embossed. The tag says whatever your imagination wants it to. The dainty lady silhouette compliments the charming gentleman. They are entitled respectively "Lady in Red," and "Man in Blue." Paintings can be purchased by writing: Terry Wilks, P.O. Box 388, Portland, TN 37148.

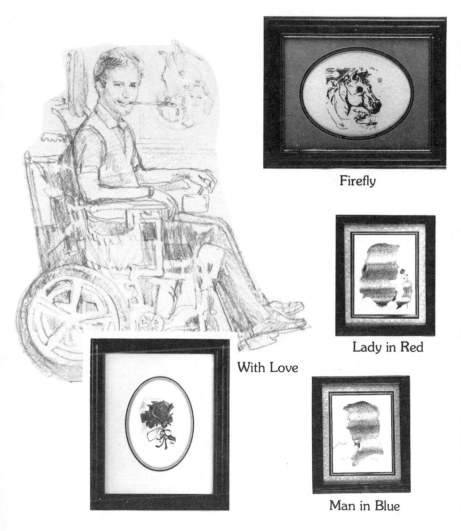

Firefly

Lady in Red

With Love

Man in Blue

Eddie, Terry's attendant, with Diane, in Bangkok, Thailand, after serving in the Marshall Islands as student teachers.

Eddie falls in love with Terry's sister Diane. They were married on June 30, 1985.

excitement in Terry's eyes that they'd seen when the van was delivered. But Terry was disappointed.

'This is my new set of legs,' Terry thought as he looked at the chair, with its wires, pulleys, hydraulic casings and tubes falling out from under the seat like a sloppy bird's nest. There was a big box on the back of it that allowed the seat to lean back to a 45-degree angle, which made it look even more cumbersome.

"Didn't they have anything that looked better?" he asked his father.

"Terry," Gilbert said, "we can take and put some pen striping on the wheels and some guards over the motors. What's important is that it's safe and it's well built. This is the best chair on the market today."

Terry nodded. He was paralyzed. What business did he have asking for a better looking chair? He thanked his Dad and apologized, but he still didn't feel right about his new chair. He would be spending every waking hour, every day of his life in this chair. If he wasn't sick, as they kept telling him, then why did he have to spend his time in a chair that made him LOOK sick. That's what he didn't like. The wheelchair looked like something that belonged in a hospital.

Learning the "sip and puff" controls proved to be one of the most entertaining times of Terry's stay at Spain. The controls were straightforward. Blow once hard to go forward, blow easy to turn right. Sip hard to stop, then sip easy to turn left. To go backwards, he had to sip hard to stop, then sip hard again for reverse. There were also three forward gears, each requiring another hard puff.

Terry's lung power was coming back slowly, but there were still times when he blew hard to go forward and instead turned to his right. Running into walls became a regular occurrence and soon staff members were hiding in mock fear, everytime he rode into the hallway. But the funniest occasion was when he sneezed, blowing the straw out of his mouth, and plowed into a row of lockers. They laughed for days over that.

Still, as he learned to control the chair, Terry began to feel a new sense of freedom. He drove around the hospital and soon became adept at turning corners and maneuvering in and out of elevators. It became a game, and the more he traveled the halls of the rehabilitation center, the more friends he made. He began to contribute more during the group therapy sessions. At Cynthia's request, he told the others about his trip home for graduation and how he'd noticed some people hanging back, not wanting to talk to him.

"That's going to happen to everybody," Cynthia said. "YOU have to take the initiative. Break the ice. Invite people to get to know you."

Terry felt a real sense of accomplishment as he came to the end of his stay at Spain. He had mastered the daily routine and made a new set of friends, with whom he had something in common.

It was going home that was hard.

The world hadn't stopped and waited for him. Five months had elapsed—five months of catching up he had to do—and other than his family, nobody wanted to slow down and help him.

His friends were all working, trying to make money for their first semester of college. They would stop by and visit but when they left he ached because he couldn't return the visit. Even though he wasn't in the hospital anymore, he was still sitting on the sidelines. How he longed to be back in the mainstream again.

Home itself had its drawbacks as well. Everywhere he looked he saw memories. Running, riding, eating, working; all of the things he could no longer do. It made him feel less human, more like a robot, and that feeling was what set off his depression. The normal routines of being human were no longer a part of his life. He couldn't even make his own decisions anymore.

When the depression became overwhelming, he painted. Working on his art was Terry's way of fighting back. No matter how long and hard it was, he wouldn't stop. He had to finish what he started.

* * *

It was Sunday afternoon. The whole Wilks family had driven to Rivergate Mall in Terry's van. It was Terry's first shopping trip since he came home. He had gone along with his family's excitement as they drove down, imagining the same kind of adventure he enjoyed on his journeys through the halls at Spain.

This time there were other people around. The sight of a pretty girl looking at him as he blew into the plastic straw made him suddenly self-conscious. What did she think? He couldn't remember ever thinking about people in wheelchairs before his accident. They were just different. Odd. Not normal. People he would never have to be concerned about. And now he was one of them.

Terry did his best to ignore the stares of other shoppers as he rode along beside his mother.

"See anything you like?" Myrna asked as they passed The Gap.

Terry stopped and looked in at the racks of shirts and pants. "Guess not," he said.

"What about a new shirt?" Myrna said. "Some of these look nice."

Terry shrugged as Myrna walked to a rack of shirts and took one off to examine. As she looked at another shirt, Gilbert joined them. "What are you getting?" Gilbert asked.

It all seemed ridiculous to Terry. Even if he bought a shirt, he couldn't put it on. He couldn't button the buttons.

"This looks good," Gilbert said, holding up another shirt.

"What do YOU like, Terry?" Myrna said.

They wanted to play a game. Everybody got to choose what they liked. Okay, he thought, looking around at the clothes.

"I like those white pants," he said.

"Great," Myrna said, walking over to the rack. "Let's see if we can find some in your size."

Terry was surprised. Suddenly he realized they actually were going to buy the pants. As the sales lady pulled out several pair of the pants, he looked at them with a new perspective, imagining what they would look like on him.

Terry became excited as they paid for the pants. When his Dad dropped the sack into his lap, he burst into a grin. He'd actually been able to choose and show some individuality. Just like a normal person.

When he drove out of The Gap somebody yelled his name. It was Sheila, one of the nurses from Memorial Hospital who'd taken care of him in ICU.

"I can't believe it," she said, leaning over to give him a hug. "It's so good to see you. You look great."

"Well, I'm still alive," he joked.

She shook her head. "It's just amazing how much better you've gotten. Everybody's going to be so excited when I tell them I ran into you."

Sheila made him promise to come by the hospital for a visit the next time he was in Nashville.

That afternoon, as they drove back to Portland, Terry wore a look of contentment for the first time in months. "I can still make choices," he said to himself as he watched the pretty summer foliage pass by his window. "There are some things I can still decide about my life." It felt so good to suddenly understand that.

* * *

It was two months after Terry moved home before the family adjusted to the new routine. At first things had been chaotic with never enough time to fit everything in that had to be done. Though Myrna was with Terry everyday and could take care of most of his needs, Gilbert still felt personally responsible for Terry's care, from changing his leg bag and bathing him to brushing his teeth and combing his hair.

Diane had given up her summer job to stay home to help Myrna with the endless needs of a family of five. Both worked hard, often late at night.

David, only two, did not understand what had happened to his brother who always had taken time after school to play with him. His quiet acceptance of Terry's injury showed in the way he would stand patiently by Terry's armrest and brush his head lightly against Terry's still hand.

Gilbert still wished he could trade places with Terry. He wanted to do anything he could to make Terry's life easier. Terry's frustrations were his frustrations. One night, he watched Terry work on his painting of the kitten. Every stoke seemed never-ending. As he watched, Gilbert clenched his own teeth. He felt the strain in his own neck from the tedious process until he couldn't watch anymore.

It had taken several months, but finally Terry finished the painting of the kitten. He had decided after graduation to give it to Joanne, hoping that in some way it would make up for the way he had treated her since the accident. The two of them had had fun visiting the summer camp where they'd first met three years before, but for the most part, Terry had felt strange around Joanne. He had tried in vain to win her love back before the accident. She'd left no doubt about how she felt. But now that he was paralyzed, she was offering that love to him unconditionally. Why?

On the afternoon when Terry presented her with the painting, Joanne couldn't keep her hands off of him. She wanted to stroke his shoulders and straighten his hair, and finally Terry became irritated.

"What do you want, Joanne?" he asked.

She looked surprised. "What do you mean?"

"Do you want to get married?"

She blushed and turned away. "Why do you have to say it like that?"

"Do you?"

"Yes," she almost whispered.

"Why?"

"I just think we're right for each other. I think we could have the best possible life together."

Terry shook his head. "I've changed," he said, watching the tears roll down her cheeks. "I still care for you, Joanne, but I don't think we should go together."

"I could take care of you," she said.

"That's not what I want," Terry said. "I can take care of myself."

The tears increased. "I'm so sorry, Terry," she cried.

"Don't be," he almost snapped. He fought so hard against his own tears and self-pity, he couldn't stand someone else's. His own emotional balance was still too fragile.

* * *

The house was quiet. It was a late summer afternoon and Myrna and Diane were in Nashville shopping for Diane's back to-school clothes. Terry was sitting in the dining room looking out at the heat and Gilbert was in his study with a copy of the *Gymnastics Safety Manual*. The question of a lawsuit had been something Gilbert had not wanted to think about. He'd tried several times in Birmingham to read the manual, but the accident was still too fresh in his thoughts. Now, however, he couldn't wait any longer. The statute of limitations gave them one year to file suit and he owed it to Terry to investigate the possibility, at least.

Ever since the accident, Gilbert had fought against blaming himself for it, or Terry, or anyone else. Now, as he looked at the manual, he thought about something Ron Case had said to him.

"It's not a question of blame, it's a question of responsibility."

He opened the book to the first page and began reading:

Safety measures are as important to gymnastics as skills. When training in a gymnastic skill is introduced, it must be accompanied by appropriate safety measures. The instructor or coach's traditional moral responsibility for the safety of gymnasts—or aspiring gymnasts—now has the force of law. Lawsuits have established the principle that the gymnastic instructor or coach must be a reasonable and prudent professional. This principle is particularly important when the instructor is developing new techniques or original skills and combinations of skills. As a courtroom lawyer has said, 'What the coach calls innovation, the court may call negligence.'

Gilbert continued to read very slowly, underlining words and sentences that seemed important. He turned the page to a section of the introductory chapter entitled "Responsibility."

The chapters which follow will point out rather dramatically the many areas of responsibility of the gymnastic instructor/coach. Never before have we been so aware of the duties of a teacher to the youthful athletes in his care.

This section is here to remind the reader that listing rules and regulations is not enough. The responsibility of the instructor/coach is to carry out such precepts. . . .

Even though gymnastics safety is everyone's responsibility, the instructor or coach must bear much of it, including the responsibility to see that others do their share: the parents, the doctor, the participant.

As Gilbert read, he was impressed with the thoroughness of

the manual's advice. There were detailed instructions on safety features to look for in gymnastic equipment, checklists on preparing the equipment for use, care and installation of mats, spotting methods, personal equipment and visual aids and charts. He was getting ready to put the book down for a while when he came to the final section on charts:

Gymnasts' attention must be called to the USGSA Gymnastic Rules poster. Recent legal cases have increased the supervisor's responsibility to make sure participants understand risks involved in an activity.

Gilbert turned the page to find the list of ten gymnastic rules. As he read the list, he became angrier and angrier until he finally stood up and walked into the dining room where Terry was sitting.

"Listen to this," Gilbert said. "This is a poster that is supposed to be displayed for gymnasts to see. These are the rules you're supposed to follow. *Number one: Caution—any activity involving motion, rotation, or height may cause serious accidental injury. Number two: Do not use apparatus without qualified supervision.* Okay, number six: *Attempt new skills in proper progression. Consult your instructor. Number seven: When attempting a new or difficult skill, a qualified spotter should be used. When in doubt, always use a spotter—check with your instructor first.*"

"Nobody ever told me that." Terry said.

"*Number eight,*" Gilbert continued. "*Dismounts from apparatus require proper landing techniques. Do not land on head or back as serious injury may result. Consult your instructor.*"

"This was supposed to be on a poster?" Terry said with anger in his voice. Gilbert nodded.

"That's not fair, Dad," Terry said. "If I'd known this I never would have tried that double flip. Especially not the SECOND TIME."

"And it also says there should always be a qualified spotter,"

Gilbert said, taking his glasses off and rubbing his eyes. He had mentioned the lawsuit possibility to Terry only once before, but they hadn't discussed it.

"Dad," Terry said, "if there had been rules like this, I would have followed them."

Gilbert nodded, knowing it was true. He had to fight the anger he was feeling.

"Does this give us grounds for a lawsuit?" Terry asked.

Gilbert shrugged. "I don't know, Terry," he said, thinking about the real consequences of a lawsuit for the first time. "I just don't know."

* * *

The summer had seemed like it would never end for Terry, but as it began to draw to a close, he realized that certain things had changed. He'd gotten stronger. He could sit up in a vertical position for most of the day. His neck was stronger, largely as a result of his painting and he'd gained back much of the weight he'd lost in the hospital.

With the encouragement of his friends, he'd also begun to feel more confidence in himself, but as they prepared to leave for college, Terry grew despondent. Most of his friends would attend Southern College, where he had planned to go as well. A recruiter from the school, Miss Remley, had visited their home to encourage Terry not to give up on the idea, but everyone agreed that leaving home so soon after the accident might be too much strain for Terry's still-fragile body.

Nevertheless, he couldn't stand the thought of being left behind. He'd fought so hard to get back in the game and he didn't want to sit on the sidelines. The more he thought about it, the more he reminded himself that he COULD make decisions about his life. So what did he want? What were his options? What could he do?

Finally, in early August, he made his decision.

"Dad," he said as they drove to the press one morning in the van. "I want to go to college."

Gilbert's thoughts had been elsewhere. "Well, Terry, I want you to go to college too."

"I mean I want to go to college this year. This semester."

Gilbert didn't say anything until he had parked the van in front of his office. Then he turned around and looked at his son.

"Terry, you just got out of the hospital."

"Come on, Dad, I can do it. It wouldn't be that different from being here. I'd just have to get an attendant."

"Let's slow down a minute," Gilbert said. "You may not even be able to get in. School starts in less than a month."

"We can ask Miss Remley."

Gilbert shook his head. "Before we do anything we need to talk to Mom and see how she feels." Gilbert was feeling hurt. Why did Terry want to leave home so bad? But he couldn't think like that. He should be thankful Terry was showing an interest in things again. He remembered what Dr. Stover had said when they were leaving Spain. "Don't baby him. Treat him just like he was perfectly healthy." It was a good sign that Terry wanted to go to college. The finances might prove a problem, but if Terry wanted to go badly enough, he'd figure out some way to pay for it.

He smiled at Terry, but when he did, he was reminded again of how weak his son still was, despite all of the gains he'd made. How could he entrust Terry's care to someone else? How could he let him go?

"Please, Dad," Terry said. "I can do it."

"Let's take it a step at a time." Gilbert replied.

*   *   *

The next two weeks were filled with activity. Gilbert called Miss Remley, who was delighted that Terry wanted to attend school that fall. She would see to it that the admissions process was expedited and she suggested they get in touch with Bert Smith, a sophomore who might be willing to serve as Terry's attendant.

Gilbert called Bert, who had known Terry for several years, and Bert agreed to visit Portland and discuss how the arrangement would work. After two days, Bert said he would take the job.

Gilbert still had his doubts, but now he couldn't say no. The excitement in Terry's eyes was contagious. Even Myrna thought it was a good idea.

"All right." Gilbert said finally. "But I think we should go down as soon as possible so Terry can get familiar with the campus before classes start."

* * *

Collegedale, Tennessee was a picturesque town on the eastern outskirts of Chattanooga, built up around Southern College of the Seventh-day Adventists. The campus was sparkling with a wild variety of flowers, beautifully landscaped lawns and shrubs, and the smell of new mown grass on the day Terry arrived with his father and Bert Smith.

The giant white columns of Wright Hall gleamed in the sun as Gilbert parked the van and got out to stretch his legs, looking up the hill at the library and classroom buildings.

Bert walked up behind him and followed his gaze. "Don't worry, Mr. Wilks," he said. "Terry can ride the elevator in Wright Hall up to the third floor, then transfer to the back elevator so he can get up there. It's a hassle but there was a guy in a wheelchair last year and he did it all the time."

"Hey!" Terry yelled from inside the van. "I want to look, too."

Terry's mind was racing with the excitement of finally arriving at his new home, but there were so many things to do before he could relax and really look around. Getting situated in his room, meeting people, learning his way around the campus. Terry's room on the ground floor of Talge Hall was big enough for three, so Bert suggested they ask his friend, Donny Duff, to be their other roommate.

For a week, the boys and Gilbert busied themselves with the painting and minor construction that was needed to make the room liveable for Terry. A special shelf was built for the telephone that Terry would use. The telephone was designed on the same principle as his sip and puff wheelchair. He could blow into a straw to dial a number, once for the number one, twice for the number two, and so on, with a pause between each number. Gilbert had learned of the phone during the months after the accident as he searched for any conveniences to make Terry's life easier.

His father had done so many things for him that Terry didn't feel like he would ever be able to repay him. But now he was ready to try living on his own.

On the Saturday before school started, the first girls started arriving on campus. Terry was excited and terrified. These girls hadn't known him before the accident, like the girls in Portland. He would be starting with a clean slate.

That morning, he put on his white pants for the first time since he'd been at school, and at 10 a.m., he, his father, Bert and Donny headed for the cafeteria on the third floor of Wright Hall. As he drove into the cafeteria, Terry looked around at the girls, scattered at different tables with their parents or in groups of twos and threes. Then he noticed several girls looking at him.

"Hey, Ter, I think you have some admirers," Gilbert said with a laugh.

Terry was already self conscious enough. Now he felt on display.

"Hey, Shirley," Bert said, waving. Then he leaned over to

Terry. "You've gotta meet her, Terry, she's great."

"Yeah?"

"Hey," Donny said, joining them. "Why don't we take the van out to the lake tomorrow?"

"Great idea," Terry said immediately. The thought of going out with a group of friends for a day at the lake was almost more than he could believe. What a change in just a month's time. He was so glad he'd come to college.

"Get me some cereal and orange juice," Terry said as the others went on to the cafeteria line and he guided his chair to an empty table. He tried not to be too conspicuous as he looked around, catching the eyes of the others in the room, then looking away. Every once in a while, someone would hold his gaze and he would smile and nod. If there was one thing he felt he needed in this new home, it was friends.

Donny and Bert sat down at the table with him, and Bert raised his eyebrows. "What do you think? See anybody you like?"

"I like them all," Terry replied with a smile and Bert and Donny laughed as Gilbert walked up.

"Here you go, Ter," he said, passing the cereal and orange juice to him. As he set the orange juice down, Gilbert slipped and the glass fell forward into Terry's lap, spilling the juice all over Terry's white pants.

"Put a napkin in my lap," he said immediately, as Gilbert tried to clean it up. Bert and Donny were laughing, trying to make a joke of it.

When Gilbert sat down, Terry spoke again.

"Dad," he said jokingly, "I think it's time you went back home."

* * *

They dropped Gilbert off at the bus station early that Sunday morning. As Gilbert watched the van drive away with his son and four friends headed for a day at the lake, he had to choke back the tears. After seeing Terry so helpless in the hospital, Gilbert was amazed at his son. He acted as if nothing had happened. Six months after breaking his neck, he was leaving home for the first time in his life. Gilbert wished he could relax, but that was too much to ask. He was leaving his son in the care of other students—boys who would have their own class schedules to keep, who didn't realize how tough it was to care for a quadriplegic. As he sat down on the bench to wait for the bus, he closed his eyes and prayed that God would look after his son.

* * *

That week before school started was one of the best of Terry's life. Everyday, Bert and Donny would round up a crowd and they'd do something together. Girls seemed to enjoy his company more than he had thought possible.

The day before classes started, Terry went to the campus store with Bert to buy books for the start of school. The shop was filled with students. Terry was straining to see the top shelf of one rack when he noticed a pretty, red-headed girl walking toward him.

"Hi," she said, smiling cheerfully. "I'm supposed to meet you. I'm Sylvia." She had a very pronounced Spanish accent and laughed when Terry looked at her curiously. "See, I'm taking this beginning English course and I have to meet three new people and write about them."

She smiled at him but Terry's attention was distracted by the girl standing slightly behind Sylvia with a soft, gentle face and honey blonde hair.

"I'm Terry Wilks," he said to Sylvia. "And who's this . . .?"

"Oh, this is my roommate Audrey."

Terry smiled and said hi.

She smiled back. "My, you have nice eyes," Audrey said,

and Terry's heart skipped a beat. He did his best to control the grin that suddenly covered his face.

"Thank you," he said, feeling the heat in his ears. "So uh. . . I mean. . . you must be staying pretty busy getting ready for school and all." She was grinning back at him.

"What year are you?" Sylvia interrupted.

"I'm a freshman," Terry said.

"Oh, great, maybe we'll be taking some classes together. Or uh. . . ." She stopped. Terry's eyes were still on Audrey.

"Are you here by yourself?" he said. "I mean. . . ."

"Oh," Sylvia said. "You want to know if she has a boyfriend. You're a sneaky guy."

Audrey's smile got bigger as Sylvia pulled her away.

"We'll see you later, Terry," Sylvia said. "We've got to go now."

Terry felt slightly stunned as he watched them leave, thinking that the chemistry between Audrey and himself had been strong enough to power all of Chattanooga.

"Bert, do you know that girl named Audrey?" he asked as they headed back to the dorm.

"I thought I saw you putting the moves on her," Bert said laughing. "Better watch out. She's a senior. AND she goes with Al. You know Al? Our resident adviser?"

"You're kidding," Terry said.

"No. She and Al have been going together since they were sophomores in high school. Tough luck," he laughed.

Terry smiled. "I'm tougher," he said.

"Uh, oh," Bert replied. "Looks like our boy's smitten."

* * *

On the first day of classes, Terry made his way through the maze of elevators and swinging doors in Wright Hall, and up to the second level of the campus. He arrived in plenty of time for his first class—English. Bert walked with him to his morning classes but by afternoon, Terry was on his own. As he rode down the hill from the math building after his last class, a couple of students from the class fell in beside him and started talking about the homework assignment. A girl friend of one of the guys joined them, introducing herself to Terry, and soon there were five people walking together toward the student center with Terry in the middle of them.

"Can I ask you a personal question?" one of the girls said, and Terry smiled.

"Please do," he said and everyone laughed.

"How do you. . . I mean, how do you study?"

"Who studies?" Terry replied, and everyone laughed. "Seriously though, I have to have someone help me turn pages and everything, but I can write with my mouth."

"You can?" the girl said, impressed.

"Yeah, I can paint, too," Terry replied and felt a surge of confidence as everyone reacted with amazement.

"Well, if you ever need somebody to help you study, I'll be happy to," the girl said with a smile.

"How about this afternoon?" Terry asked, ignoring the cracks of several of the guys. He was loving it. All of the attention they were showering on him was almost too good to be true. College was turning out to be a great time.

* * *

Of all the guys Terry met in the first month, the nicest was Eddie Nolan. They had the same Bible class and Eddie went out of his way to help Terry get around.

"I know who you are," Eddie said the first day they'd talked. "I was on the gymnastics team at Mt. Pisgah, and we sent you a get well card in the hospital."

"Yeah, I think I remember," Terry said.

Eddie started coming by Terry's room in the afternoon and helping him with all the little things that needed doing. He also introduced Terry to a lot of his friends. Eddie was one of the most popular boys in the freshman class and soon most of his friends were Terry's friends as well. And it was Eddie who also rescued Terry from his first big scare in the men's room.

It had been early one afternoon and the dorm was deserted. Terry had driven his chair into the bathroom to see if Bert was there. As he rounded the corner, he bumped the wall which threw him against the left armrest of his chair. He couldn't get to the straw and the chair drove into the wall, pinning him there.

At least there's a wall, Terry thought, imagining what he would do if there was nothing to lean against. He'd be draped over the armrest and all the blood would be running to his head. No doubt about it, he was a lucky guy. But what was he going to do? There was nothing he COULD do, except wait for someone to come in and rescue him.

After thirty minutes, Terry began to panic. What would he do if nobody came? What if they didn't come in time? He might have some trouble breathing. How would he handle it? But he couldn't let himself think about that. Somebody was going to be along shortly. They had to be. This was a restroom in a college dorm. "Doesn't anybody urinate around here?" he said outloud, laughing to himself. He had to make himself laugh. He couldn't let the fear control him. Fifteen minutes later, he'd fallen asleep.

"Terry!"

He opened his eyes and saw Eddie staring down at him. "Are you okay?"

Terry blinked once to get his bearings. "Yeah, I fell asleep."

"I thought you might have been hurt. How long have you been here?" Eddie asked, pulling Terry away from the wall and setting him up straight in the chair.

Terry looked at the watch on his right wrist. "Two hours,"

he said, then smiled in his mischievous way. "I guess I was constipated."

Eddie laughed as Terry started out of the bathroom.

"Are you crazy?"

"Come on," Terry called back to him. "Let's go get something to eat. I'm starved."

* * *

The episode in the bathroom was the first of many occasions when Terry found himself alone, in need of assistance, and helpless to do anything about it. It happened several times in Wright Hall as he attempted to maneuver his chair out of the elevator without assistance. The door would close on him, bump the chair which knocked him to one side and made it impossible for him to use the sip and puff mechanism. He would be stuck there until someone else came along, and that could be a matter of minutes, or hours.

But someone always came along, and gradually Terry learned to wait without panic. He would fall asleep sometimes, but usually he simply sat and waited, thinking about all of the things he wanted to do.

As September came to an end, Terry was enjoying himself as much as he ever had. He traveled around the campus freely now, and everyone seemed to know him. To his friends, he was Terry, to everyone else, he was "the kid in the wheelchair." When he went from one class to the next, there were usually four or five people with him. When he sat out in the sun on the patio beside the student center, others would always sit down with him.

At first, Terry had been shy about asking for help at meal times, but he quickly realized that people—girls especially— actually wanted to be asked to help him. They seemed to enjoy feeding him. Terry had become a social lightning rod on campus, and although Bert and Donny began to express concern for his health, Terry would not slow down. He was having the time of his life and he didn't want it to stop.

Best of all, he was going out with girls. Donny had introduced him to his girlfriend's roommate, Terri, and they'd gone out several times. He had also started seeing another girl named Susan, Eddie Nolan's ex-girlfriend, who fed Terry one day at lunch and asked him out the next night. Susan was a cute girl and Terry was very much attracted to her, but since that first day at the Campus Shop, his most serious attention had been focused on Audrey. Maybe she was a senior and maybe she was dating his resident advisor, as his friends liked to remind him, but that didn't change the way he felt, and it didn't seem to change the way she felt.

One day he was "walking" across campus with Eddie and another friend, Reg, when Audrey came out of the girls' dorm and started walking towards them. All three of them were suddenly conscious of how they looked and when Audrey said hello, they each did their best to charm her. But when she looked at Terry, there obviously was a special spark between them. He talked to her for a minute, flirting slightly, and when they said good-bye, Eddie and Reg looked at each other appraisingly.

"Man, Wilks, I'm going to start taking lessons from you," Reg said, and Terry just smiled and blew into his straw.

* * *

Terry started calling Audrey at night. Actually he'd call Sylvia to talk about some homework assignment, then innocently ask if Audrey was around. When she'd get on the phone, the sound of her voice was like a tonic for him. She was so sweet, so loving. She never talked to him about Al, but he could tell that she wasn't happy with him. The fact was, Terry was falling in love and the time had come to do something about it.

The hassles of painting had taken away from the pleasure it had given him. However, he decided to finish the picture of the steeple he had started in art class, and give it to Audrey as a present. He hoped she liked it. The next step he had planned was to ask her out on a date; maybe on his birthday.

Each day he labored patiently with brush in mouth, slowly forming the steep, pyramid-shaped outline with the cross at the top. The painting had a three dimensional look that he was especially proud of. Everyone in the class complimented his ability, except his teacher, who seemed to be even tougher on him than he was on the rest of the students.

But the fact of the matter was that the steeple looked good; better than a lot of the other students could have painted with their hands. Like Linda told him at Spain, once the image is on the paper, it doesn't matter who put it there, or how. The important thing is getting it on paper.

Terry was driving out of Wright Hall on a late September afternoon with the painting in his lap, on his way to give it to Audrey, when he looked up and saw Audrey and Al, coming out of the girls' dorm holding hands. Terry quickly turned his chair toward his dorm, hoping she hadn't seen him. How humiliating.

He watched out of the side of his eye as Audrey and Al got into her car and headed out the main drive of the campus. He felt like a real dope, looking down at the painting in his lap. When Terry looked up, Susan was coming out of Wright Hall.

"Hey, Susan," Terry said. She ran down the ramp to say hello.

"What's this?" she asked, taking the painting out of Terry's lap and holding it up. "Where'd you get it?"

Terry watched the car drive away with the beautiful blonde in the front seat.

"I painted it," he said, turning back to Susan. "Art class."

"You painted this?" she exclaimed. "Terry, it's beautiful. I can't believe you did it."

Terry smiled at Susan. "You can have it if you want. I'd like you to have it."

Susan was excited. "I'll put it in a frame," she said.

"Listen, Susan," Terry said, feeling impulsive. "My parents are coming in next weekend for my birthday. How would you like to go out to dinner with us? Be my date and all."

"Oh, Terry, I'd love to," she replied.

"Great. We'll probably go some place like the Sailmaker for dinner."

Her smile exuded affection. "I can hardly wait."

* * *

PORTLAND

When he returned home from Collegedale, Gilbert had vowed to himself that he wouldn't worry about Terry. The dean at Southern College promised to keep a close watch on Terry and give Gilbert regular reports on his progress. In their first few phone conversations, the dean had been extremely complimentary of Terry's attitude. He was fitting in better than anyone could have expected. In fact, when one young girl had come to the dean complaining of depression, he'd sent her to Terry for counseling.

But in recent weeks, the dean's tone had changed. Terry was pushing himself too hard, staying out late, trying to do too much. "He needs to slow down," the dean had said, and Gilbert promised to speak to Terry about it. When the dean called a week later, he had become seriously concerned. "If you don't do something about it, I'll have to," he said.

"Terry's birthday is October third, and we'll all be coming down," Gilbert said. "I'll talk to him then."

Terry's condition was not Gilbert's only concern. The time for filing a lawsuit was running out and a decision had to be made. As he considered what to do, Gilbert was torn. No matter how many times he re-read the *Gymnastics Safety*

Manual and considered the lack of supervision at the time of the accident, he still hesitated. What was morally right?

In his search for an answer, Gilbert decided to contact another young man who had suffered an injury very much like Terry's. He too had faced the decision of suing. Perhaps he could help Gilbert make his decision.

The young man lived in Washington, where he was about to graduate from college after six years. He, too, was a quadriplegic.

After Gilbert told him about Terry's injury, he said: "I think you should go through with the lawsuit."

He told Gilbert of his experience and of the legal process that followed. He had won his lawsuit.

"It doesn't just involve your son," he said. "This is going on all over the country. Kids aren't getting proper instruction in gymnastics. It's not safe."

When Gilbert said good-bye, the young man wished him good luck. "Whatever you do, go through with this lawsuit," he said. "If I'd gotten word out about what happened to me, your son's accident might not have happened."

* * *

OCTOBER 3, 1981

Collegedale woke up to a cool, sunny morning. Fall was in the air and the Wilkses were up early, looking forward to a big day. They would meet Terry for church, then out to the lake for a picnic lunch and that night a surprise birthday party was planned at the Sailmaker Restaurant in Chattanooga. Two of the girls who helped Terry with his studies had planned the party.

The oak and maple leaves were just beginning to change color and they danced in the chilly breeze as the family filed into the chapel for worship. Gilbert and Myrna smiled with pride as they sat down in the pew next to Terry, who was seated in the aisle. He looked wonderful. The lines of fright and fatigue that once seemed permanently etched in his face were gone. He looked happy and everyone they met went out of the way to compliment Terry, and welcome them to the campus.

When the service was over, several students stopped them, including one very pretty girl.

"This is Susan," Terry said.

"Oh, it's nice to meet you," Myrna said. Terry had told them that Susan would be his date that evening.

Terry's excitement over his birthday was obvious as they drove to the dorm so he could change clothes. What his family didn't know was that Terry had a special reason to be happy. That morning before church, Audrey had called to wish him a happy birthday. Terry's heart raced as they talked on the phone. He told her how much he wanted to see her that day. She said she'd like that, too. And he invited her to the lake with his family for the afternoon.

As they drove to the lake, Terry was so excited he couldn't talk. Susan was fun, but Audrey was something special. She was wearing jeans and a ski jacket and her hair was as beautiful as anything he'd ever seen.

Myrna brought out the birthday cake when they got to the lake. Gilbert lit the candles and Terry was able to blow them all out with the aid of a brisk wind. Then Audrey came over to place a napkin in the neck of his shirt and he couldn't keep his eyes off her. The napkin blew to the side several times and each time, she stopped to set it right. Her hands were a woman's hands and her smile glowed with its own warmth.

"Let's go down to the boat ramp," Terry said after they finished the cake. He and Audrey started down the path alone.

They talked about school for a while before Terry asked her about Al. She shrugged.

"I don't know," she said.

"You deserve someone better than that," he said.

Then she told him how much she admired his attitude

toward life. She felt very happy around him, she said. Terry rode ahead of her, feeling the wind on his face and the incredible warmth of the sun.

"I didn't know I could feel this good," Audrey said as she laughed happily.

"Come on, jump on the back and let's see if we can pop a wheelie," he said. Audrey grabbed on to Terry's jacket and rode with him down the hill, balanced on the hydraulic casing. When she got off, they walked along the water's edge in silence for a while.

"You know, Audrey," Terry finally said, clearing his throat. "This is hard for me to say, but these last couple of months. . . I mean, well, I feel a lot for you. You're very special to me."

She was leaning over, resting her hands lightly on his arm. "Really?" she said when he finished. "I had no idea you felt that way."

They walked on and again she was quiet, communicating with her eyes and her smile, until the spell was broken by his Dad.

"Time to go," Gilbert shouted. "It's past five."

Terry couldn't believe it was that late.

"Please can't we stay a little longer," Terry begged. He looked at Audrey and her smile said everything he wanted to hear. How could he leave?

Finally Gilbert got everyone back to the van and they headed back to Collegedale. It was a long drive and by the time they got back to campus, Gilbert was ready for a nap himself. But it was already 6:30. Susan had been waiting for thirty minutes.

They dropped Audrey off at the back door and went to the front for Susan.

Saying good-bye to Audrey had left Terry very frustrated. Even when Susan came out in a beautiful dress, looking as pretty as he'd ever seen her, he couldn't get his mind off

Audrey. They drove to his parents' motel, so they could change clothes and freshen up. Susan was talking to him as they sat in the lobby and suddenly Terry wanted to kick himself. He'd already had one wonderful date that day, and his second was about to begin. How many other guys spent their 19th birthday that way?

He couldn't take this for granted; he'd fought too hard for the chance to have it. This was his LIFE, and today was a glorious day.

By the time his parents were ready to go, Terry had Susan laughing at everything he said.

"Where do you want to go?" Gilbert asked as they headed out of Collegedale.

"Sailmaker," Terry answered. "They've got the best baked potatoes in town."

"What about that Mexican place?" Gilbert said mischievously.

"Sailmaker, Dad," Terry demanded.

When they arrived, Terry didn't understand why the waitress escorted them to the very back of the restaurant. When she opened a door, suddenly there stood Eddie Nolan.

"What are you doing here?" Terry asked.

"Suprise!" Eddie replied, and suddenly there was pandemonium as Terry rolled into the party room with everyone singing "Happy Birthday to You."

They'd caught him totally by surprise and he loved it.

"Bring on the music," he said, and everyone laughed. It seemed like every girl in the room wanted to feed him a piece of cake.

"Let me get your picture with Susan," Gilbert said, and Terry smiled happily with Susan sitting in his lap. Then Renee was beside him. "I want my picture with Terry," she said, and Gilbert laughingly obliged her. Later, when Gilbert was standing off to the side, Renee approached him. "You know," she said, looking back at Terry, "that guy gives me hope.

Sometimes I feel like if I could be around him all the time, life would be good."

Gilbert smiled at her and looked at Terry.

"And I just can't STAND it when all those other girls are around him," she said, and walked off to join the group. Gilbert looked after her, shaking his head in amazement. He looked around the room, at all the others and at the decorations. A huge birthday poster hung on one wall and a net of balloons was waiting to be released from the ceiling. Such an outpouring of love for his son. It was something he had never imagined.

After an hour Audrey arrived with Sylvia, her roommate. Audrey wore a maroon velvet suit with her hair up and Terry wanted to cry with happiness when he saw her. She came over to him shyly. "Al found out I went out with you today and he took my car. That's why I'm late."

"You're kidding."

She smiled at him, and he looked around quickly at all the people. "I wish we could talk," he said. "Let's get together tomorrow."

She nodded.

"Hey, Dad," Terry said, turning around to his father. "How about getting a picture of me and Audrey."

When he said it, he realized Susan was standing right beside him, but it didn't matter. He was too happy.

But his Dad wouldn't take the picture.

"Come on, Dad," Terry said, but his father made a strange face at him.

"Dad, don't make a fool of me," Terry said under his breath and his father leaned forward.

"Pay attention to Susan," he said.

Terry backed away. "Dad, it's my BIRTHDAY."

His father looked away and Terry turned back to Audrey. "I guess we'll have to wait to get our picture taken."

The party continued and Terry kept the jokes coming. The

balloons were let loose from the ceiling and one of them landed on Terry's head.

"Leave it there," he laughed, and everyone laughed with him.

When they finally left the restaurant, Terry still had the balloon on his head.

Sylvia came up to him when they got outside. "Call us when you get home," she said, and he could see Audrey standing behind her at a distance, looking the other way.

Terry did his best not to be rude to Susan on the ride back to Collegedale. He wanted her and everybody else to be as happy as he was. He wanted his parents to be happy, and not feel like their son couldn't enjoy a normal life because he was paralyzed.

"You know," he said. "I don't think I could have had this much fun tonight if I wasn't in this chair."

He smiled at Susan and she smiled back, stroking his arm.

When they had dropped off the family and said good-night to Susan, Gilbert and Terry made their way back to Terry's room and Gilbert prepared to get Terry ready for bed.

"Dad, I want to call Audrey," Terry said. "Would you mind dialing the number?"

Gilbert sighed. "Terry, it's time to go to bed. It's after midnight. I'm so tired and she's probably asleep."

"It'll just take five minutes. I need to make sure she's okay and set a time to get together with her tomorrow. She had a rough night, Dad. She broke up with her boyfriend."

"Not tonight," Gilbert said. "Call her in the morning."

"Dad, I have to say something to her tonight. I told them I'd call. Please. If it takes any longer than five minutes, you can just hang up."

As he spoke, Bert and Donny woke up from their half dazed napping.

"Please dial the number, Dad."

"Terry, I'm just not going to do that."

Terry glared at him. "Why not?"

"Because you need some sleep; the dean says you going to ruin your health if you don't get more rest. And I'm so tired, that's why."

"You're doing this just because I'm in this chair," Terry said, his voice shaking. "I'm not asking you to do anything but dial a number."

"I'm just trying to help you," Gilbert said. He looked at Bert and Donny who were lying on their beds. Bert nodded at him. They were all exhausted. "You need your rest, Terry," he added.

"Dad, let me live a little bit of my own life."

Gilbert pushed back the covers on Terry's bed. "I'm your father and I know you need more rest. You've been up after midnight every night this week. We're both worn out and I'm not going to pick up the phone for you."

He pushed Terry's chair toward the bed and prepared to lift him out.

"Dad," Terry said, his voice breaking as he fought the tears. "You are out of line. You're stepping on my private territory and telling me how to live my life. And I have a right to ask you not to do that."

"Terry, I'm thinking about what's best for you. I'm tired. The guys are tired. It's time we all went to sleep."

"What do you have against Audrey?" Terry demanded.

"Nothing," Gilbert said. "She's very nice, but she wasn't your date tonight."

"Look, Dad, I think Susan's great too, I just don't happen to be in love with her. Why can't you let me do what I want to do?"

"I'm trying to do what's best for you. It's time to go to sleep."

"You have no right to control my life," Terry said angrily.

"Look," Gilbert said, "you controlled my life, our lives when you were in the hospital. Now I'm going to control yours a little bit. You're going to listen to me. I have my life to live too. I have to get some rest."

His father's remark had stung Terry. "You didn't have to be with me in the hospital all the time," Terry said.

"That's not true," Gilbert said. "You know I had to be with you. I wanted to be."

Terry cried himself to sleep that night, and the next morning, he woke up with a bitter feeling in his heart. How was he supposed to live his own life? Everybody wanted him to feel normal, but no one wanted him to be himself.

That afternoon, Terry was supposed to go to a banquet with Susan, where he was scheduled to be a featured performer on the program. He was going to play "Country Roads" on the harmonica, accompanied by John Robison on the banjo.

Terry wasn't looking forward to the banquet, especially after the night before, and he wasn't ready for the telephone call he received as he was getting ready to leave.

It was Audrey. She was calling to tell him that she and Al were getting back together. Terry's anger was ready to erupt but he held it in check. If only they'd let him make his call last night.

"Why?" Terry asked Audrey, and she kept giving him very cut and dried reasons.

"Listen, I've got to go now, but please think about this some more and let's talk about it. I just don't understand why you want to do it."

"I just think it's best," she replied weakly.

"I'll try to call you when I get home."

When they hung up, Terry went straight to his drawing board and took out a pencil. He began writing down reasons why Audrey should not go back with Al. He stopped when he had ten reasons, and he finally left for the banquet.

It was a wonderful evening. The Arrowhead Country Club was beautiful and the late afternoon sun lit the grounds with a warm red glow. Two hundred students were in attendance and "Country Roads" was met with warm applause.

Terry got home that night at 2 a.m. and decided to wait til the morning before calling Audrey. Then at 3:30, the telephone rang. Bert answered it and lay the phone on the pillow beside Terry's head. It was Audrey.

She was sobbing. "I don't know what to do," she cried, trying to catch her breath. "Terry, the boys' dean has been telling me I shouldn't be dating you because I could hurt you. He says it could be bad for your health. Al said the same thing. He said you haven't fully recovered from the accident. And the girls' dean was up here tonight and she told me the same thing. I just don't know, Terry. Am I hurting you?"

"Listen, Audrey," Terry said calmly, "The boys' dean and the girls' dean and all those other people shouldn't be telling us what to do with our private lives. This is just between you and me."

"You're right, everybody's telling me what to do and I don't know what to say to them." She blew her nose. "I told Al today that I love you."

Terry caught his breath.

"Oh, no, I shouldn't have told you that." She started crying again.

"Audrey, listen, I feel strongly about you too. I just think we should do what WE want to do, not what everybody else wants us to do. Let's talk about it tomorrow."

"Okay," she said. "I'm glad I called you. Did I wake you up?"

"No, no," he said, "I'm glad you called too."

That night, Terry went to sleep with a smile on his face. It felt so good in so many different ways. He felt the heady sensation of every man who has won the heart of the girl of his dreams. He'd followed his feelings, and in the end, he'd prevailed. He felt his decision was a mature one. This wasn't some temporary infatuation that would blow over once reality set in. There was something deeper between them.

He believed that night that if he ever lost Audrey, it wouldn't be because they hadn't loved each other enough. He knew that love was there.

* * *

For the next month, Terry and Audrey played a game of hide and seek around the Southern College campus. Audrey could not simply ignore all the people who were reminding her daily that her relationship with Terry could only end up hurting him.

So they met at odd hours in strange places. They would be seen late in the evenings down by the tennis courts, or in the library early in the morning.

The hours started taking their toll on him, not to mention Bert, who was becoming less and less understanding about Terry's new schedule. Donny had moved out because of the constant interruptions of his studying. Somehow, Terry managed to keep up his studies, but his mind was on Audrey.

It was all right with him that she needed to keep a certain privacy about the relationship, as long as she looked at him with those same loving eyes.

But the comments of everyone else were making it harder and harder to stay together. Audrey had told her parents, and their voices were added to the chorus of people telling her she was making a mistake to date a handicapped boy. Terry wouldn't give up though. He loved Audrey with his language. He did everything he could think of to keep her close.

But slowly she slipped away.

Her parents came for a visit before Thanksgiving, and Terry felt a chill of disapproval more strongly than ever. They all went for a ride in his van, but when they got back to the campus, her parents walked on to the dorm and didn't wait for him. And Audrey seemed ready to cry.

So Terry stopped calling her. If she wasn't interested

anymore, he wasn't going to pursue her and make a fool of himself. But she was interested, that's what he couldn't stop thinking about. He knew how he felt and he knew he'd felt the same thing from her.

Finally a week before finals, Terry called Audrey for the last time, and asked if they could get together and talk. It was a cold afternoon, and Terry was bundled up, as they sat in a quiet corner of the student center. "Audrey, I feel so much for you. I love you. I know I'm in a wheelchair. I know your parents disapprove, and there are a lot of others who disapprove. But I can't help feeling this way."

She looked down at her hands.

"As far as our future together, I don't know if I can be a good husband someday. I don't know if I can support you or not. All I can promise is that I'll love you and I would like us to be together until we find out if we have all the things it takes to get married."

Audrey was quiet. Terry kept talking and slowly she began to open up to him and talk about her own, real doubts about their being together. Could they have a family? Could they have the kind of intimate relationship that husbands and wives normally enjoyed.

"I don't know if I can live without that, Terry," she said.

He didn't know how to respond.

* * *

The whole fall semester had grown more difficult as it neared its conclusion. The rigors of studying without being able to take notes; of having to write out the answers to test questions with his mouth; of having to keep pages and pages of information in his head were taxing him more than he let anyone know. The physical demands of it were exhausting.

And the cold weather made everything harder. It wasn't so bad at first. Terry could sit outside for hours and not even feel cold. But when the chill finally hit him, it went to his bones and stayed with him for hours. Many were the nights that Terry came back to his room and had Bert cover his whole body with every blanket in the closet, and even then it took two hours before he stopped shaking.

He was getting less and less sleep, losing weight, looking pale. Yet he kept going.

"Come on," he would shout to his friends as they crossed the campus and came to the top of a small rise. He loved speeding ahead of them on the downgrade, feeling the wind in his hair. "When I get out of this chair I'm going to show you all how to ride a horse," he'd yell and everyone would laugh with him.

Finally, three days before final exams were to start, Terry woke up in the morning coughing blood. The first diagnosis when they got to the emergency room of Erlanger Hospital was pneumonia, but after the initial tests came back, the doctors informed Terry that he was suffering from tuberculosis.

* * *

The quarantine sign on Terry's door had frightened Gilbert at first, but the nurse assured him Terry was doing fine.

"He'll be ready to leave in another week or two," she said.

Gilbert smiled. "I guess he's just been having too much fun."

Gilbert had come down by himself to be with Terry. The doctors said it would not be wise to expose the rest of the family to him, especially with Christmas coming up. They recommended that Gilbert take Terry someplace warm for the holidays, once he was released.

As he walked into the room, he could feel the tension that was left over from the birthday party. Terry was polite, but distant. Gilbert stood by the bed and they talked about what had happened since he'd arrived at the hospital. Terry was very anxious to be discharged.

"Everybody's real nice to me, I just don't like hospitals anymore," Terry said.

Then Gilbert told him the big news. He had spoken to an attorney in Nashville, Hal Hardin, and the lawsuit would be filed before the end of the year.

"That's Great," Terry said.

"Hal Hardin has been a judge and former United States District Attorney in Nashville," Gilbert said. "He's one of the best lawyers in town."

"I'm glad we're doing this, Dad," Terry said, and Gilbert nodded. He wasn't exactly glad about it, but he believed it was the right thing to do morally.

They talked about what they were going to do for Christmas. Gilbert suggested Miami, but it was such a long drive. Finally, Terry said what he really wanted for Christmas was a T-bar control for his chair, that he could manipulate with his hand. His shoulders were strong enough now that he could move his arms and he was tired of the sip and puff mechanism.

Gilbert called the company in Montgomery, Alabama where he'd bought Terry's chair, and they agreed to install a T-bar control system for him. And so, Gilbert began making arrangements to spend Christmas with Terry in Montgomery, away from the family, and all the things he had looked forward to. Terry, too, seemed depressed about missing Mom, Diane and David. So much had happened. He couldn't believe that only 14 months ago, the family had spent the holidays in Wyoming, riding ski mobiles through Yellowstone Park.

There had been so much pain. Even though they had made it through the worst part, there was still pain. Everyday. Gilbert thought about spending a week alone with Terry. It would be hard on both of them, but that was all right. As long as he could be close to Terry, he felt he could handle things.

Feeling Alone

SUMMER 1982

The gym was set up just as he'd seen it dozens of times in the past with seats in a semicircle around the mats. His expression remained unchanged as Robbie Elliott stepped up to the parallel bars and swung into a handstand. Around him, people applauded. Terry held onto his composure desperately. How could he watch this?

When the vault box was moved into the middle of the floor, Terry could no longer hold his emotions in check. The tears collected on his eyelids and began to roll uncontrollably down his cheeks. "Mom," he whispered. When Myrna turned around, Terry was already headed for the door of the gym.

It had been a mistake to bring Terry to the Home Show, she realized as she hurried to catch up with him. But he'd said he wanted to be there.

"I'm so sorry," she said when they were outside.

"Don't worry about it, Mom," he sniffed. "Just wipe off my face, would you?" She put her arms around him as he cried. "It hurts so bad," he whispered, and she began to cry too.

As they drove home in the van, Terry stared out at the thick summer foliage along Old Fountain Head Road, wondering if he would ever be able to watch a gymnastics event again. Maybe on TV, but not his friends. Not now, at least. It was too much like going to his own funeral.

The whole summer was starting to feel that way. In fact, the whole year. His fight against the negative thoughts had intensified during the second semester at Southern College, as the novelty of being "the kid in the wheelchair" had worn off.

The tedious repetition of his daily routines—suppositories every other day, three-hour sessions with his attendant every morning just to get ready for school, the regular trips back to the hospital for minor infections—eroded his self confidence the way a river washes away its bank. Slowly. Insidiously. And every day he had to shore it up with nothing but his own courage. The fight for life wasn't as intense now as it had been in the hospital, but the fighting continued everyday, inside his mind.

Was all of the fighting worth it? That was a question he had stopped asking himself because the answer was always the same. He believed the fight was worth it. That was the first article of his new faith.

But even so, it was hard. Losing Audrey had changed Terry. Her vision, her presence in his memory gradually disappeared, but left behind was an attitude that made everything look a little darker, less vivid, less important. The love of his life didn't love him. He would never find anyone who would care as much for him as Audrey had cared. So he believed.

It had been easier to handle when he was at school, surrounded by his buddies, but now he was alone with his loss.

One good note at the beginning of the summer was that Eddie Nolan had agreed to come home with Terry and serve as his attendant. Eddie and Terry had become best friends, and Diane also was happy about the arrangement. She had gone out with Eddie several times during family visits to Collegedale and they had become good friends. In fact, the whole family was excited.

But Terry's attitude soon began to change, as his friend warmed to his new role in the family. Eddie began working at the press during the day, helping out with chores around the house on weekends, mowing the lawn, washing the cars— doing all the things that Terry had done. And Terry observed it all with a growing jealousy.

At least he had the vacation to look forward to. Gilbert had sent off for information from the National Spinal Cord Injury Association, and had received the schedule of events for the upcoming NSCIA Convention in Minneapolis. There would be seminars on home health care, diet, wheelchair technology, sex, medical advancements and a wide range of other topics of interest to the physically disabled. Terry was excited about attending the convention, so Gilbert had planned the family vacation around it. They would all drive up in Terry's van to the Wisconsin Dells for a week of fun and relaxation, then on to Minneapolis. Everybody was looking forward to the trip. It would be like old times. A family vacation together. It was just what they needed.

* * *

THE WISCONSIN DELLS—SUMMER 1982

"Gilbert, could you get those last two bags," Eddie said as he came in the front door carrying an armload of luggage. Myrna and Diane were already in the kitchen of the condominium, looking for cooking utensils and little David was exploring the bedrooms.

"Isn't this a beautiful place?" Gilbert said as he headed back to the van for the last two bags.

"We need to go find out where the parasail place is," Eddie

said to Myrna. "I can't wait to see you try that."

"No way," Myrna said and Diane immediately started kidding her. "Come on, Mom, you have to try it."

"Now don't start that. Go on out and explore."

She shooed them toward the door laughing.

"See how much it is to rent a ski boat," Gilbert yelled back to Eddie as he came inside. "Boy, the mosquitoes are bad here, but isn't it beautiful? Don't you think so, Terry?"

Terry sat in his chair by the window, watching Eddie and Diane run down the path toward the lake. He looked at his father, who was wiping the sweat from his forehead. "Yeah, Dad, it's beautiful," Terry said.

He turned back to the window and watched as Eddie took Diane's hand and they walked out of view, smiling at each other.

"Terry, what's the matter?" Gilbert said. "You've hardly said anything since we left home. Why are you being so quiet?"

"It's just the way I feel," Terry replied turning away from the window.

"I wish you'd be more a part of the group," Gilbert said, stealing a glance at Myrna.

"I guess I just don't feel like that right now."

"Well, why don't you drive into the market with me. I have to go get groceries," Myrna said, but Terry shook his head.

"I'd really rather just go in my room for a while."

Terry sat alone, wondering what he was going to do for the next five days. Why couldn't they have gone some place where there was action—where you didn't have to do something physical to enjoy yourself? Terry thought about the family vacation they'd taken before his accident, to Yellowstone Park in the winter of 1980. He, Diane and his Dad had rented snowmobiles and taken off racing across the virgin powder with the wind and the snow in their faces.

That was the kind of vacation his family had always taken,

so why should this be any different? Maybe he wouldn't enjoy himself, but everyone else certainly would.

"Whatcha doing?"

Terry turned around to see David, standing in the doorway with his finger in his mouth. He was three now, and he still seemed a little afraid of Terry's wheelchair.

"I'm looking at the trees, what are you doing?"

David shrugged.

"You gonna go swimming?"

David shrugged again and picked up a tape recorder sitting on the bed. "I don't know."

Terry smiled at him. "Where's your coloring book?"

"I don't know," David said again.

"Go get it and I'll watch you color," Terry said.

"I want to go see Mommy," David said. He put the tape recorder back on the bed but it fell on the floor. He ran out of the room.

Terry looked back at the trees, thinking about how much he wished he could run to his mother and have her make everything all right. How he envied David and his innocence. How he wished he was a child again, without responsibility. When he watched David draw in his coloring book, Terry could see himself. He could remember how he loved to lose himself in his drawings. But now, he knew, the real world didn't allow such irresponsibility.

Then he heard Eddie and Diane come back inside. The sight of them holding hands had been a shock to him. There was no doubt that she and Eddie were becoming more than just friends.

Just then, Eddie came into the room. "The lake is beautiful," he said dropping onto the bed. Then he noticed the tape recorder on the floor. "What's this doing here?" He picked it up and turned it on, but nothing happened. "How did this get knocked on the floor?"

Terry shrugged.

"David," Eddie said loudy, and a few seconds later David appeared in the doorway.

"Did you knock this on the floor?"

David looked scared.

"Did you?" Eddie demanded.

"Hey!" Terry suddenly said. "You don't talk to my brother like that. You're not a member of this family."

Eddie was taken back. He didn't say anything else and after a moment, he left the room.

Terry looked back out at the trees, wanting to cry, feeling more alone than he'd ever felt in his life. He cared for Eddie, he liked what was happening, but he needed the same thing.

* * *

It all seemed to have come down on him at once. All of the depression, the frustration that he had forced himself not to think about, suddenly engulfed him, and he was fighting it alone. While the others went skiing or parasailing or swimming in the pool, Terry remained alone with his thoughts.

He was, in a very real way, experiencing the living death of disability. He thought to himself that if he were left alone with everything he could possibly need to survive for the rest of his life, he would die in a matter of days. How many other people in the same circumstance were spending their lives alone. A lot of them, he knew. Without some independent source of money, disabled people were forced to live on workmen's compensation, disability checks, welfare. There was no way for a quad to pay full-time attendants on that income.

He knew how lucky he was to have a father who loved him and had enough money to pay for his care. But ultimately for Terry, that meant that his father had the power to decide how he lived his life. For example, his father decided where Terry would go on vacation. Because of his disability, he had different interests than his parents now. He liked to watch television and listen to music. His parents liked an active life.

It became very clear to Terry as he sat alone in the beautiful lake country of Wisconsin that if he was to have the life he chose—which was the one thing he realized he truly wanted— he would have to become economically independent. And that was going to take a fight equal to the one he won in the hospital. It was the same fight: to stay alive.

* * *

The more he was alone to think, the more Terry began to lose himself in the elaborate and expanding world of his own thoughts. Mental discipline had been a goal of Terry's for three years before his accident, and since the accident, he had been forced to work even harder at controlling his mind and focusing his concentration. He had been too busy to stop and think about it, but now, sitting by himself in the quiet of the Dells, he began to see just how far he had come. He saw his mind as a muscle and he realized that all his efforts to develop it and make it stronger were beginning to pay off.

It was on a warm morning, while everyone else was down at the lake, that Terry decided to write his first poem. It would be a song—about David, about growing up, and about the end of innocence. And it would be months before he finished it in his mind and finally committed it to paper. When they finally left the Dells, Terry had turned his attitude around. And now he was ready for the excitement of Minneapolis.

* * *

Terry was on an expedition, exploring every corner of the hotel for different activities. He wanted to know where every seminar would be, where every booth was set up for display, what was for sale and for how much. And his first objective was to see what was going on in the area of wheelchair design.

He had owned his own chair for more than a year now—first with a sip and puff mechanism, now with a T-bar—and he was ready for something different. The chair was okay for someone right out of the hospital, but not for the long term. It was too uncomfortable. The seat was slick so you tended to slide on it, and moving the armrests was so much trouble that it was simpler to leave them in place, even when that made getting him in and out of the chair almost impossible.

But when he went into the display of home health care products, no one knew of any new wheelchair products on the market.

"The ones we've got now seem to work pretty well ," one young man told him. "Don't you like your chair?"

"No," Terry replied. "It looks like it belongs in a hospital."

"But it works, right?"

"So does a hospital gown, but you don't wear it in public." The young man laughed.

It was more than just not liking the way wheelchairs looked. Terry resented the attitude that looks weren't important. People who wore a certain kind of clothes, parted their hair a certain way, and who in general were quite attentive to their own appearance, were telling him that the way he looked was not important. The chair was his legs. Of course he cared what it looked like. And it wasn't that he wanted something fancy, just something that looked GOOD. And felt a little more comfortable. Surely a chair could be functional without looking clinical.

The second afternoon, coming out of a seminar on home health care products, Terry saw his father talking to a woman with a clipboard, who seemed to be one of the main organizers of the conference. He decided to drive over and find out who she was.

She was Louise McKnew, a newly appointed fundraiser for the NSCIA and one of the driving forces behind the convention. Louise had a son named Donnie who was Terry's age. When he was 18, Donnie's car had gone out of control on a gravel curve and he had been paralyzed from the shoulders down. What was worse, he had remained in constant pain since the accident, three years before. Searching for some way to help her son, Louise had dedicated her life to finding a cure for Donnie and others.

"Your father tells me you paint," she said. "That is wonderful, Terry. I'd love to see some of your work."

Terry nodded, wishing he had something to show her. The fact was, he hadn't painted anything in a year. "What does your son do?" Terry asked.

"Donnie's a sophomore at Yale," she said.

They started talking about the seminars and Louise suggested they check out one session on pharmaceutical developments.

"Do you know about Naloxone?" she asked. Naloxone was a drug that had excited those concerned with spinal cord injuries more than any other. If administered within the first several hours after an accident, Naloxone could prevent the formation of scar tissue in the cord, thus allowing the nerve endings to remain in contact and preventing paralysis.

Naloxone's side effects had proved difficult to control, however, and another drug called TRH—Thyrotropic Releasing Hormone—was beginning to look like the new drug of hope. It did the same thing as Naloxone, but with different side effects.

"The only problem is that these drugs have no effect if they aren't administered almost immediately after the accident," Louise said. "But it seems to me that if they can arrest the paralysis process, they can learn how to reverse it too. That's what I dream of. It's like I told Donnie, 'If man can place his foot on the moon, someday they'll discover a way for you to put your feet back on the ground.' "

She told him the NSCIA was beginning an effort to raise $100,000 to support additional research.

"That doesn't seem like a lot of money," Terry said.

"It isn't," Louise replied. "But it is for this kind of research. We have to get the word out."

Louise had an idea for a fundraising brochure entitled "STEPS: Steps To Ending Paralysis." She was thinking about turning it into a nationwide campaign. The problem, once again, was money.

As Gilbert began talking to her about the possibility of Wilks Publications becoming involved in the fundraising effort, Terry decided to look around some more.

One seminar he had been very interested in from the first time he saw it mentioned was one on interpersonal relationships. As he'd hoped, the seminar turned out to be about sex, the one thing he truly wasn't sure about. He still thought about the therapists at Spain, telling him he had a sexuality, but how much of a sexuality? All he wanted to know was truth.

And what he heard boggled Terry's mind. Individuals with spinal cord injuries could still have sex. In fact, quads had more success than paraplegics, because their injury was higher on the spinal cord.

Quads have a priapism, Terry learned, which meant they could sustain an erection. Sperm had to be surgically removed, however. But if the sperm was still fertile, a quad could become a father. It was possible.

The leader of the seminar showed a film clip of a young man in Michigan, paralyzed from the neck down, who had married and fathered a child by artificial insemination. He was a Catholic and the church had opposed the birth, but the man had stood by his decision.

When the seminar was over, Terry was in a state very much like shock. All this time, he had believed that it was impossible to father a child, impossible to enjoy the pleasures of sex, impossible to have a family. Now, suddenly, it appeared all of those preconceptions were wrong. Maybe he really would have a wife and a family after all. The thought transported him with happiness. It made him feel more human.

* * *

As the week went on, Terry realized that almost every major person involved in advancements for spinal cord injury victims was in attendance.

There was Dr. Jerrold Petrofsky's chief assistant. Dr. Barth Green from Miami was also there. He was the doctor who was having researchers from all over the world fly in so he could evaluate their work. These people were involved in research aimed at improving the lives of paralyzed people. Terry felt compelled to meet them all.

Petrofsky's experiments at Wright State University in Dayton, Ohio sounded most remarkable. A young paraplegic named Nan Davis had actually "walked," with a system Petrofsky invented to send eletrical impulses from a computer to the muscles in the legs through electrodes. Much remained to be done, but the film of Nan Davis taking her first steps was an exhilirating sight for those in attendance at the convention.

A similar type of research was being conducted at the University of Miami by Dr. Green, who was using biofeedback as a way of stimulating muscle response. Dr. Green's research wasn't as dramatic as Petrofsky's, but the results were beginning to draw attention. If Petrofsky was the eccentric genius of the profession, Green was the respected professional.

Indeed, there was an excitement about the advancements for the disabled that Terry had not experienced before. It was as if every research project was on the verge of a breakthrough, and all they needed was for the rest of the world to embrace the cause. But Terry also observed a very realistic attitude on the part of the professionals. For all their optimism, they knew how hard money was to come by, and they knew the speed of their breakthroughs depended entirely on the size of their cash flow.

By the last day of the convention, Terry had become a part of this much larger family. As he went around and talked to other people in attendance, he began to realize that the talents he possessed opened up avenues beyond those he'd imagined. His drawing talent had seemed a minor source of pride, but after he learned about the Association for Handicapped Art, it had become a potential livelihood.

That last afternoon, Terry decided to go down to the hotel jacuzzi. When he got there, he found it occupied by a group of people, all of whom suffered from Multiple Sclerosis. At first, Terry thought about leaving, but he overcame the urge and instead drove up to the side of the pool.

"How's the water?" he asked.

"Nice and hot," one of the men replied.

"Just the way I like it," a woman added.

They talked until the group got out of the jacuzzi, and Terry left feeling good. It had been hard at first, hard to overlook those aspects of their appearance that weren't normal. But once the ice was broken, it had been easy. They were normal people inside, no matter what they looked like outside. Just like him. And he had truly enjoyed their company.

* * *

What had begun as a difficult summer ended for Terry with a new sense of purpose. He had two goals. The long term goal was to become financially independent. The short term goal was figuring out how he was going to do that. At such times, he would think fleetingly of his lawsuit. If only. . . . But he knew he couldn't start daydreaming about that because that was killing time and he had no time to kill.

He also had learned some things during the summer about

himself and his family. He was growing apart from them. Because of the accident, he was developing different interests. He was beginning to see the world in a different way than he saw it when he was still the old Terry, and he sensed that his family still wanted the old Terry back.

Eddie had seemed to take the place of the old Terry. And as much as Terry wanted his new life, they were still his family and he couldn't help being jealous.

Terry asked Robbie Elliott to be his attendant once school started back up, and he looked forward to that. Robbie was a great friend.

It was a different Terry Wilks who arrived on the campus of Southern College in the fall of 1982. There was still a sense of joy, but it was tempered now by a realist's vision of what lay ahead. A year before, he had seen himself as just another kid on campus, determined to be treated normally. Now he knew he wasn't. No more jokes about what he was going to do when he got out of the chair. No more chasing after girls who enjoyed flirting but couldn't get past what other people thought. That didn't mean he was going to stop flirting, just chasing.

The girl who caught Terry's eye those first weeks of the fall semester was named Mauri. He had spoken to her the first day of classes, and invited her to Student Assembly, but she didn't really pay him any attention. When he asked her out again, she was busy.

"That's too bad," Terry said to her. "But listen, the next time you're free, give me a ring."

Terry lived in the same dorm room he'd lived in his freshman year, and a lot of his old friends came down to visit. Mark Decker's brother, Steve, came down a lot. Terry had gone to Mark's wedding at the beginning of the summer in Arkansas, and their friendship had continued to grow when Mark moved to Portland after the wedding to go to work for Wilks Publications. When Steve would come down, they would talk about Mark and about his artwork, and the more they talked, the more Terry began to think about his own art.

One day, Steve brought it up. "Mark always said you were talented," Steve said. "Do you ever paint anymore?"

Terry hesitated a second, then nodded. "Yeah," he replied.

The next day Robbie set up drawing paper on his board and sharpened his charcoal pencil. He already knew what he was going to draw. It was a man's head, a Roman gladiator type. The previous semester, he and Mark had talked a lot about a technique that uses only dots. The pointilist method. Terry wanted to paint a pointilist gladiator's head.

That first day, as he formed the outline of the head with dots, he remembered the old sensations—the way it felt to SEE the picture before you paint it, to feel the lines flow from the pencil as if it had a mind of its own. Those sensations had not been a part of drawing for him since the accident. It had been purely hard work.

But now as he continued to put dots on the paper, he realized it had become easier for him. His neck was stronger so he could control the pencil better, and he'd become accustomed to the perspective. Drawing by hand gave the artist a two-foot perspective, whereas drawing by mouth gave you six inches. It was like looking at a drawing through a fish eye lens.

After four hours, he had finished the basic outline of the character, and begun to fill in the facial features, when Robbie finally came by to see what he wanted to do about dinner.

"What are you doing here, Wilks, trying to mess up this paper?" Robbie said, looking skeptically at the half finished drawing.

"Just wait 'til I finish," Terry replied.

He would always remember the feeling he had as he neared the completion of his first drawing. It was like running a race and knowing you're going to win. The momentum was there, the flow. No matter how long it took, he knew he was going to finish it and get it right. A wave of happiness washed over him everytime he pulled back from the drawing and saw what he was creating.

When he showed it to Mauri, at first she didn't believe he'd done it. "Come on, where'd you get it?" she said.

"It's a Picasso," Terry joked.

"Come on."

"I did it."

"Seriously?"

"Seriously."

She looked at it again. "This is really good. I mean, it's REALLY good." She looked at him and broke into a smile. "You're an artist."

"That's what I've been trying to tell you," he replied.

"Paint a picture of me," she said excitedly, and Terry laughed happily. Maybe there really WAS a future here.

And so Terry's interest began to shift to art. It had been almost two years since he'd really spent any time at all drawing, but now it was coming back to him as if he'd been away from it for two days. He was good at it, he knew, if only he had more time for it. His daydreams were not so much about girls anymore. They were more about success.

* * *

It had taken Gilbert two months to develop the STEPS brochure and deliver it to Louise McNew. He was proud of it. Pernell Roberts—Trapper John—was featured on the cover, as was Terry as a representative of the 20,000 Americans who were paralyzed each year. "Don't take your steps for granted . . . take steps to end paralysis."

In the fall, Gilbert flew to Washington on business, and stopped by Louise McNew's office to talk about plans for distribution of the brochures. She was enthusiastic about what he'd done.

"Things are looking good," she told him. "We're moving into a new building at Christmas."

They talked about their sons and Gilbert's eyes began to mist up.

"It's all right," she said. "I know how it feels. You keep thinking it's going to get better, but it doesn't. It gets worse."

Gilbert nodded. "It sounds stupid, but I really wish I could trade places with him. That's what I want to do."

"Me, too," she smiled.

Louise asked Gilbert about the lawsuit, which he'd mentioned to her before. "Gilbert, you've got a moral responsibility to follow through, for Terry's sake and the sake of those who might get hurt in the future, if safety isn't improved. And do you know, it costs at least a million dollars to sustain a quadriplegic for their lifetime."

Gilbert shook his head. "That's so much money."

"Not when you consider that if Terry's brain had been injured—which was a distinct possibility—the cost of his care would be twice as much."

They talked about Petrofsky and Barth Green and Gilbert mentioned that he would like to visit both places, to see if there might be some way Terry could be involved in their projects.

"Speaking of Petrofsky, Mike Wallace from 60 Minutes is in Dayton right now, doing a story on Nan Davis. Why don't you go down there now. You could meet Petrofsky AND Mike Wallace."

Gilbert laughed. "I couldn't just barge in and announce that I wanted to meet Mike Wallace."

She had already picked up the telephone. "I have a friend with CBS. Let me give him a call."

"But what can I say to Mike Wallace?"

"Tell him about Terry," she said. "Terry's a remarkable kid."

It wasn't until Gilbert had his seat belt fastened and the plane for Dayton was taking off that he stopped and realized what he was doing. He didn't know what to say to Mike Wallace about Terry and he had an hour to come up with something.

He took out paper and pencil and got himself situated but when it came time to start writing, he didn't know what to say. "Dear Mike."

He stared at the words for ten minutes. Maybe he should invite him to Portland or Chattanooga, or maybe he should suggest that Terry meet him someplace. The important thing was for them to meet. But what if he was asked why? What made Terry special enough to be interviewed on 60 minutes?

As he thought about it, the tears began to come to his eyes again. He was thinking about Terry's attitude. That was the thing that set him apart. The attitude that he shouldn't feel sorry for himself. That he could do whatever he set his mind to.

He was happy and self-confident and full of life. He made people feel better about themselves. How could Gilbert express it to make Mike Wallace understand.

Gilbert looked up and was embarrassed to see that the young woman beside him was smiling. She introduced herself and asked him why he was going to Dayton.

"I'm going to try to meet Mike Wallace. . . ." Gilbert began, but she interrupted him excitedly before he finished.

"So am I. He's interviewing my sister."

"Really? Nan Davis?"

"Yes," she beamed at him. "You know, as soon as I got on the plane I felt drawn to sit beside you and I didn't know why."

For the rest of the flight, they talked about Nan and Mike Wallace and Terry, and when they got there, Gilbert still hadn't finished his note to Mike Wallace, but it didn't matter because Mike Wallace and the whole "60 Minutes" crew was just leaving, and her parents asked Gilbert to watch her bags while they ran to see if they could catch them.

Gilbert looked at the note as he waited at the baggage claim area. 'One day, I'm going to finish this note,' he thought. But not for Mike Wallace. For himself.

* * *

Terry sat at the window on the third floor of Wright Hall, staring out at the snow blanketing the campus. Christmas was coming on, which meant Terry could be found most afternoons by his favorite window with "the best radiator on campus." A good radiator AND a seat in the sun were two of the great pleasures for a quad in winter. Another reason he liked the spot was because it was right on the way to the restroom, and everyone always stopped and said hello.

Today, Terry was going to be interviewed. His friend Blaine Pleasants was going to pick him up and take him into the News-Free Press Building in Chattanooga. It was for an article to run Christmas Day, entitled "Christmas Angels."

As he looked out at the sun gleaming off the top of the girls' dorm, Terry felt like anything but an angel. He was feeling hostility and anger and wishing more than anything that he could lash out at something, somebody, rather than sit like a bump on a log and brood. Loneliness was suicide for a quad, and Terry was feeling very lonely.

His whole focus that fall semester had become his art. After the pointilist Roman gladiator, he had painted a rose for Mauri, and he liked it so much that he kept the original for himself and made her a copy. It had taken him 40 hours of work.

Then he painted a picture of Mauri petting a horse, but after he gave it to her, they gradually stopped seeing each other. He didn't mind that so much, because he started seeing her friend, Rochelle. But so far, all he knew about Rochelle was that they got along well. Very well sometimes.

Then he and Robbie had a falling out. When Terry had completed four drawings, which were well received by everyone who saw them, he decided to try and sell copies of them to make some spending money for Christmas. He went to the campus print shop and had some copies made and then got Robbie to put up a display in the girls' dorm, offering the pictures for sale.

But nothing sold, and when Terry finally asked Robbie to go back and take down the display, Robbie became angry.

"I'm not your slave," he said.

"Robbie, this is what we're paying you for, to help me do things I can't do."

"You're paying me to take care of you, not run your errands. I told you you shouldn't have put that thing over there anyway."

"Look, Robbie, just go take it down."

Finally he'd done it, but the tension hadn't eased. Terry was beginning to wonder if it was possible to have a friend as an attendant. First Eddie, now Robbie. He'd gone through the same thing with Bert. Sooner or later the line between friendship and employment was crossed, and usually it was the friendship that suffered.

Probably the thing that made him the lowest was the fact that the pictures didn't sell. When he thought how hard he'd worked on those pictures and all the people who had told him how good they were, he couldn't understand why they hadn't sold. Maybe people just didn't like HIM as much anymore.

Maybe he should try to be more like the person he used to be, before the accident. No. He couldn't do that. He knew it immediately. He would just have to be who he was and let other people worry about whether they liked him or not.

"Hey, you ready?"

Terry turned around to see Blaine. It was time to go to be interviewed. He just hoped he could find something interesting to talk about.

CHRISTMAS ANGELS

By Ida Jayne Hoye

Chattanooga News-Free Press Staff Writer

They are always there. They make life special every day.

There's a warm smile, a friendly "hello" and a special sense of compassion. Some have had a few hard knocks. Others realize how precious life is and make the days of others easier to handle. They are in a sense "angels"—messengers showing all of us the goodness in young people. . . .

TERRY WILKS was a high school senior when he attempted a double flip as a gymnast and landed on his head, bruising his vertebrae. This stopped signals to the brain and left him paralyzed.

"We were all amazed at his emotional strength and faith after the accident," said Mrs. Phil Robertson, whose husband was associated with Terry's school at the time. "Before the accident he was always positive and the kind of student teachers appreciated. He also showed a lot of courage throughout the ordeal."

In the fall after the accident, Terry Wilks came to Chattanooga and entered Southern College. That first day was hard as he wheeled through a cafeteria filled with 600 students, most of whom were "staring." There was no movement in his hands and he had to blow into a device to trigger the movement of his motorized wheelchair.

Terry believes "That we are not just left alone down here. God has a hand in our affairs. A person has to try to make the best of each circumstance he has and take personal pride in his abilities and personality and try to develop that to the utmost. Life IS what you make it."

Terry has the use of his arms to some extent now, but he has started painting through the use of his teeth. Some pieces have already taken as many as 85 hours but he perseveres. Friend, Blaine Pleasants, who works with Terry in physical therapy, admitted with a chuckle, "He's always very positive except when he's having GIRL problems. He has taught me to be appreciative of what I have and he helps keep me feeling good at times and vice versa."

Terry has learned a lot about people since the accident. "You learn where they are coming from. You get to where you can see behind their makeup and come to understand why they are the people they are. So many times we wonder about defenses that other people have and it's because we set up stereotypes.

"It's when we try to understand their unique makeup—what makes them cry; what makes them shy—that we can come to see them. In most people there is a reason for the way they are. We may not like the way their lifestyle is as compared to ours, but we still can look and accept them for what they have been through and how they reacted.

"The hardest thing to go through is rejection from someone else. When you come to realize your own internal values and become your own friend, then you can make yourself smile when it's raining. It's then that you can start seeing other people's internal values."

By the time school let out for Christmas, Terry and Rochelle were dating seriously. In fact, Rochelle was joining him and his parents for their trip to Washington to attend the NSCIA Christmas Fund Raising party and the dedication of the new national headquarters building for the Paralyzed Veterans of America.

Terry had been looking forward to this trip because his father had learned that a number of corporate sponsors of NSCIA would be on hand and Terry wanted to meet them. He'd read recently about a quadriplegic going to work for IBM and he wanted to find out if there were any special programs for the disabled.

The gala NSCIA Christmas party was a formal affair, and Terry took a special pleasure in the tuxedo he'd rented for the occasion, especially when he saw the other people there his age, some dressed in street clothes. Rochelle was impressed too, when they were introduced to several Congressmen and a vice president with IBM.

"We'd be very interested in talking to you about a position with IBM," he told Terry. "We have a young man working for us now, a quadriplegic, making $25,000 a year."

"Really?" Terry said, looking at Rochelle with surprise.

They saw Gilbert talking with Louise McKnew and another young man in a wheelchair, and went over to say hello.

"Terry, I want you to meet my son Donnie."

They said hello and talked for a moment before Don left to rejoin a group of his friends.

"It's hard to believe that Donnie's in pain alot," Gilbert said, and Terry nodded.

"I don't know how I could handle it if I was still in pain," Terry said.

Louise was about to cry. She turned to Rochelle. "What you have to understand, Rochelle, is that what happened to Terry happens to an average of sixty people a day. Twenty thousand a year. That's as many people as used to get polio. One day their life is in the palm of their hand, the next day it's totally out of their control.

"That's why we're here tonight. There's a lot of things we can do for these people, if we have the money."

She turned and smiled at Terry. "By the way, have you stayed in contact with Dr. Petrofsky?"

"Well, I went to visit him," Gilbert interjected. "He's invited Terry up sometime maybe later this spring."

"Oh, you should do that," Louise said. "What about Barth Green?"

"We've written him a letter."

"You should visit both of them," Louise said. "They are doing incredible things with muscle regeneration and they need people like you. Strong people with good attitudes."

* * *

They left for Tennessee that night when the party was over, everyone taking in their last glimpse of the beauties of Washington as they headed south in Terry's van.

"Did you have a good time?" Terry asked Rochelle, who was sitting beside him on the couch in the back of the van.

"Yes," she smiled.

He leaned forward and kissed her. Then again. And again.

"Hey, Dad," Terry said after about thirty minutes. "You said we'd have to get to a motel by about midnight?"

"Yeah?" Gilbert said.

"Do you think you could drive on for a couple more hours?"

Gilbert grabbed Myrna's hand and squeezed it. They laughed. "Yeah, I guess so," Gilbert replied.

* * *

They made the trip to Petrofsky's over Spring Break. By that time his research had been featured in *U.S. News and*

World Report and the "60 Minutes" segment was about to air. "We are trying to liberate people from wheelchairs," was the caption under the picture in U.S. News.

The weather had been terrible on the trip, cold and wet, with patches of unmelted snow dotting the urban landscape. Their motel was next door to a truck stop with the only restaurant in the area.

By contrast, Wright State University was a very pretty place, with carefully landscaped grounds and buildings that were all wheelchair accessible.

The first day they visited, there was no one in the bio-engineering building, and they were wandering down a dimly lit hallway when they heard voices behind an unmarked door.

There, in what looked like a cross between an electrician's shop and a small gymnasium, was Jerrold Petrofsky's lab. There didn't seem to be an empty surface in the room. Every shelf was covered with transistors, sensor pads, computer screens, potentiometers, electrical equipment of all kinds. And in the middle of the room, leaning over a desk, was Petrofsky.

He was a big friendly man with an unsophisticated nature, who, like Gilbert, loved to fly. They talked about airplanes for a while, and then Dr. Petrofsky invited Terry to sit with him and discuss his research.

"It's another way of getting the message to the legs," he said.

Electrodes were taped to the skin over paralyzed muscles in the legs and a computer was programed to order successive bursts of electrical stimulation to produce walking. A similar system made it possible to ride a tricycle.

Terry was fascinated by the system but not because he wanted to try it. For one thing, it required upper body movement. The system was for paraplegics, not quads. And for another thing, it scared him. As he watched the film of Nan Davis walking in that jerking motion, he kept thinking about what she would do if the computer short circuited. In terms of movement, it was a success, but he questioned its value in terms of mobility.

"I just don't think a computer can account for all the situations you meet when you're walking," he told his father that afternoon when they were back at the motel. "It's like they're playing without all the safety procedures."

They returned to Petrofsky's lab the next day and met Nan Davis. She and Terry hit it off right away. She was getting excited about seeing herself on "60 Minutes", and Terry told her he'd have to draw a picture of her, now that she was going to be famous. She liked that. She told Terry about her life at Wright State and all of the ways in which Dr. Petrofsky's research project had made her life better, and what Terry liked about her was that she talked about normal, human things. There was no "wheelchair talk," as he called it. Just typical conversation between peers. And, she was cute.

They stayed in Dayton for three days, and by the time they left, Terry knew he didn't want to return as a part of Dr. Petrofsky's team. He liked the people, but he was looking for a different kind of activity.

"Like what?" Gilbert asked as they drove home.

"I don't know yet, Dad."

"Maybe you'll like Barth Green's better," Gilbert said. "I understand they're more into exercise and conditioning down there."

"Dad, I'm not sure I want to become a part of somebody else's experiment."

"Well, Terry, we need to talk about this, about what you're going to do. With Diane in college, that means two tuitions. I know you've said you aren't that happy with college. Maybe there's something else you'd rather do?"

Terry shrugged. "Dad," he said, "do you ever think there will be enough money? I know all this expense is more than we can afford. I guess what I'm wondering is, do you think we might get a settlement from the insurance company?"

Gilbert shook his head. "It could take years, Terry, and there's no guarantee that we'll win. They're just now starting to take depositions. We just can't count on that."

There was a heavy silence as they drove south. Terry had known that his Southern College tuition, medical expenses and attendant care, was expensive, and they'd talked before about what he was going to do after he finished his sophmore year. But the reality had not really set in until now. He was going to have to find something new to do with himself. What it was going to be, he didn't know.

* * *

Several weeks after they returned from Ohio, Gilbert called Terry to say that he'd contacted Barth Green in Miami and there was a possibility that Terry could join his program for the summer.

"We need to let them know something now," Gilbert said.

Terry wasn't ready to make the decision, so Gilbert suggested they go ahead and accept, then they could drive down at the end of school and check it out.

By the time the school year ended, it had been unofficially decided that Terry would move to Florida for the summer. He had talked to Bert Smith, his first attendant who had relatives in Miami. Bert agreed to serve as Terry's attendant. It was only a question of where they would live, once they got down there.

* * *

After the fun they'd had the summer before, Gilbert and Myrna thought it would be a good idea to plan their family vacation around Terry's trip to Florida, and invite Eddie Nolan.

By the time they left for Florida in the van, Terry was feeling almost exactly the same emotions he'd felt the summer before—left out and isolated. When he asked them to turn on the radio, they said no, they'd rather talk. But Eddie was doing all the talking, and everytime he spoke, the rest of the family acted like it was an E.F. Hutton commercial.

So Terry shut up. He held it all inside, his anger growing with each passing mile, until they arrived in Ocala, Florida and he finally let it out.

They were all in the parking lot of their motel in Ocala, unloading the van, and Terry was staring off at nothing in particular when Gilbert walked up to him.

"What's the matter with you, Terry?" he said. "You're becoming such an introvert. It just seems like all you think about is yourself anymore."

The dam inside Terry broke.

"How do you know what I'm thinking?" he demanded. "You don't know anything about me anymore." Tears had come to Terry's eyes and the others in the family stopped what they were doing, nervously hoping that there wouldn't be a scene.

"Everytime I try to say something, you shut me out. You don't listen to me, Dad. You're not helping me develop in the way I want to develop."

"Now that's not true, Terry. I do listen to you."

"Nobody in this family listens to me," Terry said, tears now streaming down his face. He looked around at the others, standing in the parking lot with luggage in their hands. "You're ignoring me, but at the same time you have complete control of my life. If I tell you what I want to do, you tell me what I should do, and THAT'S what I end up doing."

"Why don't we go inside?" Gilbert suggested and Terry shook his head angrily, as Myrna walked over and put her hand on Terry's shoulder.

"He's right," she said. "We don't listen to Terry the way we should."

Finally Terry calmed down and they went inside. He felt bad because he'd become angry, and did his best to be a better family member, but in his heart he was glad he'd said what he felt.

When they arrived in Miami, Terry was already dreading his visit to Barth Green. He was sick of being told that some doctor's research was going to make him better. It was a dream, a fantasy, and he couldn't live with that fantasy and still have a life. His job was to deal with reality.

Dr. Barth Green's lab at the University of Miami was a first class operation. There wasn't that sense of a maverick inventor Terry had felt on his visit to Petrofsky. The facilities were bigger and cleaner and the procedures looked a lot safer.

Dr. Green, like Petrofsky, was experimenting with electrodes as a means of stimulating muscle response in paralyzed limbs. But his focus was not to enable someone to walk again. Instead, he was using the system as an exercise devise, to keep the muscles from atrophy. He was also spending a great deal of time researching nerve regeneration—and using biofeedback as a means of muscle exercise.

It was fascinating to walk through the laboratory and see the various activities going on as a part of the research. Several paraplegics were working on the biofeedback machine and when they finished, Terry asked if he could try it out.

They connected sensors to his shoulders, and by moving certain muscles, he could control the ball that was in front of him on the TV screen. The object was to make the ball go to the top of the screen, and if possible, off the screen, thereby bringing up a more difficult program.

"It's a way of getting more control of your muscles," the assistant told him.

He liked the biofeedback machine. He could see how useful

it could be in building muscle control.

Terry was very impressed when they left that afternoon, but he'd also made up his mind he didn't want to stay.

"I just don't want to be involved in a long-term experiment," he told his father. "There are a lot of interested people and I think this could really help their lives. But it's not for me."

"Well, what do you want to do?"

"I want to make some money."

"Terry, you can't be too choosey."

"Why not? Why can't I choose what I want to do?"

Gilbert thought about it a moment. "Maybe you could go to work at the press?"

Terry nodded, realizing that that probably was the most realistic option he had right now.

"Yeah," he said. "That might be the best thing."

* * *

But before he went to work for his father, Terry wanted at least one more try at doing what he wanted to do.

Terry's energies had been focused more and more on his painting. He hadn't been able to spend that much time on it the second semester, but he still had five paintings that were good enough to put on display. Maybe he could do something with his art. While they were in Florida, Terry and Bert started talking about things they could do together, to make money. One day, when the whole family had driven to Orlando, he and Bert went to the Fashion Square Mall and began discussing the possibility of opening an art and frame shop. The more they talked about marketing and sales techniques and the type of paintings they would carry, the more excited they became about the idea. It was a fantasy, but it was fun.

Could it be a reality, though, that's what Terry wanted to know. Joni Eareckson sold her artwork and had become very successful. Maybe he could repeat her success. He knew that whatever he did, it was going to require his father to put up the front money. So he began to see his goal as finding something that wouldn't require a lot up front, and would make enough so that he could pay his father back and be on his own as soon as possible.

*   *   *

Gilbert and Terry had been planning for months to attend the Abilities Unlimited convention for home health care products in Anaheim, California, that spring. Terry had become insistent about buying a new wheelchair, and they were going specifically for that purpose. But Terry had also found out that Joni Eareckson would be there and he was hoping to have a chance to talk to her about her art.

Gilbert had business in Florida the first day of the convention, so he let Terry and Bert fly out ahead of him. It was an exciting trip for Terry—his first airplane flight since his accident. Then having a day at the convention "on their own" was even more fun. Terry loved driving in and out of the rows of booths in his chair, looking at all of the creative things people were inventing to make life easier for the disabled. There were new types of vans with driving equipment for the disabled; there were computerized, handicap accessible video games; there were new types of elevators and beds, new leg bags and wrist splints. There were even displays of other people's art.

For Terry, the most impressive booth in the whole exhibit hall was Joni's. Her artwork was prominently displayed, along with copies of her books—*Joni,* and *A Step Further*— underneath a large, hand-carved wooden sign that said: "Joni and friends." There was a TV monitor playing the movie about her life. Paintings for sale. Cards. Calendars. She had worked very hard to create what she had created, Terry realized. Joni Eareckson was an industry.

This was what he wanted. He wanted to carve a niche for himself, the way Joni had. Not work in a laboratory as the subject of someone else's experiment, but make it in the real world—the walking world. That's what Joni had done. Her first book alone sold over a million copies. She was a real success in real terms.

"Your stuff's almost this good," Bert said, looking at a painting for sale.

"This is what I want to do, Bert."

When Gilbert arrived the next day, Terry had already begun plans to start a business. He was going to become a full-time artist. Bert was going to work for him. All they needed was the start up capital.

Gilbert smiled at Terry. "And how much is that going to be?"

"I don't know yet," Terry replied. "I'll tell you when we've got our prospectus finished."

The rest of the convention was great fun. Gilbert arranged for Terry to meet Joni. She was very nice and looked at some of his paintings.

"These are good," she said. "If you'd like, I'll send them to my publisher."

"Great."

Terry even found a wheelchair he liked. It was called a Quadrachair, very fast and good looking, but he felt it was unstable.

Other than that, though, the only new wheelchair was something that looked like a miniature golf cart, with big tires and a fiberglass body encasing the works. They would have to wait on buying a new chair until Terry found something he really liked.

Wheelchairs weren't as interesting to him now, anyway. He was about to embark on his new career as an artist.

Where Do We Go From Here

SUMMER 1983

The Creekside Apartment complex was a big, sprawling place, located about a mile from the Opryland amusement park on the eastern perimeter of Nashville. A lot of kids who worked at the park lived in the complex. Maybe that explained why there always seemed to be music playing and people around the pool. It was a great place if you were young and looking for excitement, and Terry Wilks was both of those.

It had been a whirlwind month since they got back from Anaheim. Gilbert had agreed to finance Terry's new business and he liked the idea that Terry would be in Nashville, close to home. He wished Terry would live at Highland, but felt it was good for Terry to try it on his own, if that's what he really wanted. Bert had agreed to come to Nashville as his attendant and employee of the company he formed—Terry Creations. Another friend from Southern College, Bill DuBois, also planned to join them.

Gilbert immediately put several people at Wilks

Publications to work on an advertising display that Terry could use to showcase his paintings in art shops and department stores around town. There were 40 shops in Nashville, and as soon as they got settled into the apartment, they would set out to make the rounds. Their approach was to sell the paintings to the art shops and department stores, and *they* would turn around and sell them to the public.

Terry would sell prints of the five paintings he'd completed at school the year before. When Gilbert went to the color separator to discuss making the reproductions, the man was very enthusiastic about the work.

"If these were hand painted, they'd sell. Being mouth painted, they're going to sell like hotcakes."

In an effort to hold down on unit cost, they decided to print 2,000 of each painting, using a new "state of the arts" laser color separator that assured the best possible reproduction. At a national framing convention in Atlanta, they arranged to buy materials and frames at cost.

If sales were as good as expected, Terry could make as much as $50,000 the first year. In any event, he was going to have to earn at least $35,000, just to pay for his care and living expenses. Either that, or he would remain financially dependent on his father.

But Terry was experiencing another sort of freedom that summer that took his mind off finances. He was on his own for the first time in his life and he relished the experience.

The first day he was there, Terry took a stroll around the complex. There was a steep hill leading from his building up to the swimming pool, but once he'd made it up the hill, he was on level ground. He loved driving along the sidewalks, smelling the rich summer odors and feeling the late afternoon sun on his back. It would have been very hard for Terry to describe the satisfaction he felt. The very fact that he was able to live away from his family and the larger family of the church was a victory for him. He'd won another round.

* * *

After weeks of getting the product ready, Terry and Bill were on the road everyday, calling on art shops all over Nashville. In some shops they were politely turned down, but in most of them, the owners were more than happy to display his paintings. One store at Rivergate Mall even invited Terry to come and paint at the store during an art show. Finally, a chance to show his stuff.

It was the end of the first evening of the show—10 p.m. on a Saturday night—and Bert was packing up the equipment. A young man had come into the shop and the owner had brought him over to meet Terry. His name was John and he, too, was an artist.

"This is very good," John said, admiring the horse Terry had drawn during the showing. They talked about Terry's work for a while and then Terry asked John about his work.

"How many paintings do you have for sale here?" Terry asked.

"About 25," John said. "I have about a hundred on consignment at different places."

Terry nodded, preoccupied by the thought of his own portfolio of five paintings.

"How did it go today?" John asked.

"It went well," Terry said. "There always seemed to be a crowd."

"Yeah, there were people around the whole day," Bert added. "At one time, there must have been at least 50 people watching you draw."

"How many did we sell?" Terry asked and Bert shrugged.

"Not too many."

"Don't worry about that." John said.

They talked for a while longer and then John said good-bye. "Good luck. I hope you make a lot of money."

"I plan to," Terry said laughing. It felt good to joke with another artist, but after he'd left, Terry's thoughts turned darker. He would have to do a lot more painting if he wanted to do it right. John had a hundred paintings on consignment. Would the fact that Terry was "handicapped" cause people to buy his paintings rather than John's? He didn't know, but he was learning fast that there was no easy way to make a living as an artist. He thought about the scuffed shoes that John wore and the old, dried out leather vest that looked like it might have belonged to John's grandfather. John was not getting rich as an artist. Terry remembered a conversation he'd had with Mark Decker back in college. "There's a rule that artists starve," Mark had said. Could he be an exception to the rule? Terry wondered.

* * *

The wheelchair strained up the path, the belt beginning to slip as he neared the crest of the hill.

"Need some help?"

It was a girl's voice, behind him.

" I think I can make it."

Then he felt himself being pushed the few remaining feet of incline and finally he was on flat ground again.

"Thanks."

"No problem."

He turned around and smiled at a pretty, brown haired girl in a bathing suit with a shirt on over it and a towel around her neck. "This chair wasn't exactly made for climbing," he said.

When she smiled, he was caught off guard by her friendly eyes.

"I'm Terry."

"Hello, Terry, I'm Lisa." Her hair was dark and she spoke

with almost no accent, She was maybe 24—an "older woman" by Terry's standards—and she had a kind of sophistication that he found very attractive.

"So you're going swimming?"

"Yeah."

"Well, come on, I'll walk you over to the pool."

They talked as they walked. When Terry told her that he was an artist, she was very impressed. She worked at a local insurance company. Terry left her after a few minutes to continue his walk, but not before inviting her to his apartment to look at his paintings.

A couple of days later, Lisa dropped by Terry's apartment to see if he wanted to join her at a Nashville Sounds baseball game. The ballpark was not wheelchair accessible so they settled for dinner and a movie.

The next day, Terry was feeling wonderful. "She likes me, Bert," he said at lunch.

"I wouldn't get my hopes up if I were you," Bert said. "That girl drives a Jag."

"I know," Terry said. "It's her boss's car."

"Doesn't matter whose car it is, Wilks. She's driving it. She's out of your league."

"Hah," he said. "I'm playing in the majors."

A week or so later, Lisa invited Terry over to her apartment, and when he got there he found her boyfriend, who had shown up unexpectedly.

"Oh, Steve, I want you to meet Terry Wilks. He's the guy I was telling you about." She looked at Terry then and made a face of apology. "Terry, this is Steve."

They sat around and talked for a while, and Terry could see that Lisa was not that happy that Steve showed up.

"Why don't we get a pizza?" Terry suggested. "Would you mind getting it, Steve?"

"Sure, I'll go."

When he'd gone, Terry looked at Lisa suggestively. "Now

that we're alone. . . ."

She laughed. "You did that on purpose, didn't you, just to get him to leave."

"Who, me?"

She came over to him laughing. "What am I going to do with you?"

Terry smiled as she kidded with him. She was nice. Maybe she would be the one? The one WHAT though? The one who would marry him? No, that wasn't it. Maybe she would be the one who wouldn't care what other people thought. That was it.

Two nights later, Terry had asked Bert and Bill to lay him on the living room floor with a pillow behind his head, so he could watch television. It was one of the first cool evenings of autumn and they'd built a fire in the fireplace. After they'd made sure Terry was comfortable, Bert and Bill had left.

Terry was feeling very satisfied. Lying by the fire reminded him of evenings he'd spent sitting by the fire at home, playing the guitar and singing with his Mom. It had been a long time since Terry had thought about his "youth"—as he called it, being all of 21 years old—his life before the accident. Terry had learned not to think of his body as something that once had life in it. The memory was simply too painful. So he thought about other things—the future mainly, and the present.

His mind had wandered off to thoughts of his painting—they were in the midst of negotiations with Cracker Barrel to display Terry's work in their gift shops—when there was a tap at the door.

"It's open," he said loudly.

The door opened slowly and Lisa looked in. She seemed shy. "May I come in?" she asked.

Terry smiled. "You certainly may."

She walked over and sat down beside him on the floor. She'd been thinking about something important but she didn't know how to say it. It was complicated but, well, she needed to talk about it.

"The problem is, I think I'm falling for you."

When she leaned over and kissed him, he wanted to cry from the desire just to be able to reach out and hold her. But she held him instead and he kissed her with an intensity that surprised her.

Lisa stopped after several minutes for fear Bill and Bert might return. "I really shouldn't get involved with you," she said, almost teasingly, leaning over to kiss him again.

* * *

After their evening by the fire, Lisa began to visit Terry four or five times a week. They would sit together in the living room watching television and talking. It was wonderful to be with her, like a game of wooing. But with his feelings, Terry was very guarded.

On her birthday, Lisa had already made plans with Steve, but the next day, a Sunday, she had accepted Terry's invitation to Opryland and dinner afterwards.

That afternoon, Terry, Bert and Bill went out and bought roses, a birthday cake, and a few other surprise items for Lisa. When they got home, Bert and Bill had an idea. They would take the roses over to Lisa's apartment, sneak in the balcony door and put them on the coffee table in the living room.

"Great idea," Terry said.

Terry followed them outside and laughed as he watched Bert slip into her living room with the flowers, then out again without them. When they got back, Terry called Lisa.

"Where were you?" he asked, as Bert and Bill tried to keep from laughing out loud.

"What do you mean?"

"I came over and you weren't there so I left some flowers on the coffee table. Happy Birthday."

"Terry, what are you talking about?" He heard her put the phone down, then she was back.

"I can't believe it. There really are flowers on the coffee table. How'd you get in here?"

"Well the front door was locked so I came in the balcony."

"Terry!" She was laughing. Then he heard Steve's voice in the background. "Well, thanks for the flowers anyway," she said.

"Aren't you going to invite me over?" he asked and she tried not to laugh. "No!" She hung up.

Bert and Bill were feeling triumphant.

"That was fantastic," Bill said.

"Yeah," Terry replied, going to the window to look up at Lisa's apartment, then back at his friends. The mischievous gleam was back in his eye. "Now we take the cake."

Lisa loved it. The next day, while they were at Opryland, Terry could almost see her changing toward him. It was becoming more than a flirtation now. It was a beautiful day and the trees had started changing their colors. Once, as they were waiting in line for a show, Terry saw a girl he'd known at school. After they'd talked for a moment and she'd said good-bye, Lisa asked him who it was.

"Oh, nobody," he said, smiling at the thought that she might be jealous.

When they went home that afternoon, there was a banner strung across the entrance to the complex. "Happy Birthday Lisa," it said.

"Did you do that?" she demanded, laughing.

"Who else?"

They went to his place, where Bert and Bill had already started preparing a special meal for the evening. And after dinner was served, and everything was cleaned up, the two guys excused themselves and Terry and Lisa were alone.

They sat on the couch and she told him how much she enjoyed the whole weekend. The flowers and the cake.

Opryland. Now a "gourmet meal."

"This is the best birthday I've ever had," she said.

Terry smiled at her. "That really makes me feel good," he said. When she leaned over and kissed him, Terry felt there had been a breakthrough in their relationship. There was a different feeling between them now. But then, almost at the instant he had the thought, she pulled back, smiling at him. "I shouldn't do this," she said.

"What do you mean?"

She shrugged. "You know."

"I don't get this," Terry said. "You tell me you don't want to get involved, then you kiss me."

"I don't know, Terry, I'm just confused. I don't understand my feelings."

"Well, I can't understand them if you can't understand them."

"I don't want to talk about it," she said leaning over to kiss him again.

Terry's feelings were not confused. He wanted more than anything to open up his heart again but he could not. Not until he knew she would do the same. But in the meantime, he was enjoying himself immensely.

* * *

At Hal Hardin's law office in Gallatin, three file cabinets had now been filled with depositions in Terry's lawsuit. In the almost two years since the suit was filed, many of those who had been involved in the school's athletic programs and those who had been in the gym on the day of Terry's accident had testified. As the end of October came on, only one deposition remained to be taken—Terry's.

For Gilbert, the lengthy delays had been nerve racking but his resolve had never wavered. He knew they were doing the morally right thing. The need for better safety regulations in the schools had become a passion with him. He could still remember the physical repulsion he'd felt that afternoon at the World's Fair in Knoxville when he'd seen the young girl practicing on the trampoline without spotters. If they could win the lawsuit, maybe that would at least be a step toward bringing about better safety precautions.

In the final weeks before Terry's deposition, Gilbert and Terry discussed the case at length. Hardin had made copies of every deposition that had been taken, and Terry spent most of his free time reading them. He read and re-read the safety manual. And for three days before the deposition, he sat in the living room of his apartment, thinking of every question the insurance company attorneys could ask him, and how he would respond.

On the day of the deposition, Terry was ready.

It was a cold, crisp October morning when Terry's van pulled up at the law offices of Bone and Ammonette in Gallatin. Terry made his way into the offices with little trouble and said hello to Hal Hardin. Gilbert was there, but Terry had asked that he not be present for the deposition. One wrinkle of his father's brow and he would have been totally distracted.

The lawyers for the insurance company were already in the conference room and when Terry entered, they all stood up and said hello. Everyone was friendly, to the point that Terry had to consciously make himself think about what he was doing there.

Once they were all settled at the conference table and the court reporter was ready, the deposition began. The first questions were simple and straightforward, and Terry fell into a pattern of listening to the questions, pausing, then responding. Sometimes he would pause for several seconds, sometimes it seemed like minutes had passed before he was able to answer

After the second hour, the questions began to wear Terry down, but he would not drop his guard. He ingnored his own memories of the emotional trauma that period had held, and concentrated on making his answers as smiple and honest as possible.

The questions continued, seemingly an endless stream of them until Terry began to feel they were running out of things to ask. He began to feel that old excitement he'd always associated with running a race he knew he was going to win. Finally, after five hours, they were finished.

"How'd I do?" Terry asked Hardin as they were leaving the room.

"You were a pro."

Terry smiled. That was good enough praise for him. "So what happens now?"

"Now we wait and see what the insurance company wants to do."

"How much longer before we know something?"

Hardin shook his head. "It could be a couple of months or it could be a couple of years. You never know."

* * *

Terry had grown tired of waiting on the lawsuit. After his deposition, he had felt a real sense of victory and he was ready to have the results, but the wait continued.

"You just have to put it out of your mind," Gilbert told him. "Don't plan on getting that money. Live your life. If God would have us win, we'll win. It's out of our hands. We've just got to keep on working hard, making enough money to cover expenses."

It was good advice, Terry knew. Putting the lawsuit out of his mind was the only way to get on with his life. But his life was not working out the way he planned. For one thing, the paintings weren't selling. There was still a great deal of interest and the art shops encouraged him to produce more paintings, so they would be able to offer a wider selection but there was still the need to be out everyday selling. And it took so long to produce a painting.

That was one thing he didn't like about it. For Terry, painting had always been a feeling thing, an emotional and artistic outlet. Now he wasn't painting anymore, he was producing paintings. It was a job, just like any other job, and he didn't know if it was the line of work he really wanted to dedicate his talents to.

He was putting a lot of pressure on himself, trying not to take it all personally, wanting to know that he'd given it his best. But he couldn't keep from asking himself the same questions, over and over. Why weren't they buying the paintings? Was it because he was disabled? Or was it because the paintings weren't good enough?

The thoughts ran through his mind until he began to suffer for it physically. He would stay at the drawing board ten or twelve hours in a row, working to achieve perfection, and after a week or two, his body began to deteriorate. His scoliosis, curvature of the spine, became worse. He looked gaunt and felt tight all the time. It was strange, but even though he was paralyzed, he could still feel it when his muscles got tight.

And he got sick. For a week, he had to stay in bed and rest. His body simply couldn't stand the stress.

Then there was Lisa. After the wonderful weekend of her birthday, they had begun plotting on how they could spend more time together alone. Lisa wanted Terry to come to her apartment, but if he did, he would need Bert or Bill to come along and help him sit on the couch. If she came to his apartment, Bert or Bill would have to be around there too.

"That kind of limits our options," Terry said after they'd discussed it one afternoon.

"I just don't want anybody around," Lisa said.

"They'll leave."

"That's not what I mean."

"Well, what do you mean?"

"Come on , Terry," she said, embarrassed. "You know what I'm talking about."

"No, I don't."

She sighed. "I just can't relax."

"You mean because somebody would know you were alone with a quad."

"No that's not it and you know it." She looked away. "Look, I've got to study for a big test I have to take at work in a couple of days. Call me tomorrow, okay?"

"You call me."

"Terry." She looked at him with hurt eyes, then left.

Terry felt lousy the next day. He was crazy to be so hard on Lisa, just because she was acting like probably any girl would act in the same situation. He hadn't wanted to fight, it had just happened.

When Bill called that afternoon on his way home from visiting art shops, Terry asked him to stop by the florist's and pick up some roses. Then Terry called Lisa.

"Listen, I'm sorry about yesterday. I was wondering if I could come over in about thirty minutes."

"Oh, Terry, now's not a good time. I'm sorry. What about tomorrow?"

"What's wrong with this afternoon?" he asked.

"I've got this big test tomorrow and Steve's here helping me study."

"I won't be there five minutes," he said.

"Terry. . . ." She wanted him to make it easy on her.

"Look, Lisa, I want to talk about yesterday and I bought you some flowers and I just want to bring them over."

"Terry, please. Steve won't be here long. He's helping me study for this test. I'll come over when he leaves."

"Great," Terry said and dropped his hand on the phone's off switch.

As he sat waiting for Bill to get home with the roses, Terry grew more and more upset. Lisa had told him that Steve was not important in her life, and now she wanted to put Terry off because Steve was there. She didn't mind Terry knowing she was seeing Steve, but she didn't want Steve to know she was seeing Terry.

When Bill got home with the flowers, Terry told him to take them to Lisa's apartment. "Give her a message," Terry said. "Tell her these flowers are from Terry, for what they're worth. And by the way, Terry doesn't want you to call him anymore."

That night, Terry felt a hardness inside of him that he couldn't let go of. He still wanted to be with Lisa, but not on these terms. He couldn't keep waiting for her to understand her feelings. When she called that night, he told her he was watching TV and asked her to call back later. When she did, he could tell she'd been crying.

They talked on the phone a minute before Terry gave in and told her she could come down.

When she got there, Terry unleashed his anger. This wasn't some game they were playing, where she got to tell him one thing, then do something else. She told him she had strong feelings for him. Was she telling Steve the same thing?

Lisa began crying as soon as Terry got upset, and when he'd finally told her how he felt, she was sobbing uncontrollably. He didn't understand. She had a major test at work the next day. If she passed it, she could move up from secretary to a claims adjuster. Steve was helping her study.

"It's more than just tonight," Terry said. "It's everything."

They sat up talking and crying until 2 a.m. Terry tried to make up. He asked her to kiss him. But everything was so confused... He knew it was his handicap that was causing it.

During the next two weeks, Lisa would call but Terry was afraid to make-up. His friends told him he was being unreasonable, but he was listening to his already-bruised heart and he simply had to do what he had to do. Maybe he would regret it later—and he did—but he had to go with the message that came from inside of him. He wanted love; total commitment, just like everyone else. Forget the chair, the awkwardness of a love with handicaps. He wanted to be normal and treated that way. He cried: "Oh, God, it's hard. I'm trying, but it's so hard."

* * *

Three days after Thanksgiving, Terry, Gilbert and Bill were driving back to the apartment after a visit to the printer. They had increased the number of prints they had on consignment around town for the Christmas season, but after that, things didn't look very promising.

"I think it's time for us to seriously look at this," Terry said. "I'm tired of not seeing any hope of making money. We're out selling everyday but no matter how good we do, we're still going in the hole. And I'm starting to think that things aren't going to change. I think it takes more publicity to promote this kind of business."

Gilbert suggested they stop for lunch, and they pulled into a restaurant and went inside. At the table, the conversation continued.

"I think we've been doing everything we can," Bill said.

"That's right," Terry said. "We're doing all we can and we're still going in the hole. And let's face it, since I'm paralyzed, I have to pay you guys and that drains the profits by $35,000 a year. That makes the feasibility of this whole thing just impossible."

Gilbert and Bill both sat quietly, considering what Terry was saying. "So what do you want to do?" Gilbert finally asked.

"I'd rather get out now, while I still have my head above water. That way I could try another project if something comes along, rather than sink on this one."

Bill turned away and looked out the window. "I don't agree," he said. "In my opinion you should never quit."

"What do you mean quit?" Terry asked. "If you were drowning because you were swimming in a race, would you keep swimming and drown or would you let them save you and train for another race?"

Bill shrugged and Gilbert sighed.

"I don't know, guys, I think there should be some way we could save it," Gilbert said.

"I'm open to suggestions," Terry said, but they couldn't think of anything to say.

"I just don't think we're drowning," Bill said. "We're selling something almost everyday."

"Let's face it," Terry said. "People like the idea of handicapped art, they like to watch me work, but they don't buy the framed paintings. People don't buy paintings, period."

"That's not true, Terry," Bill said. "Look at that guy we met at the art show that night. John."

"Yeah, and he's broke. It's like Mark told me back in school. 'Artists starve.' And I can't afford to starve."

They stared down at their hands for a moment, then Gilbert spoke. "So what do you want to do?"

Terry shrugged. "Can I go to work at the press?"

"Sure," Gilbert said. "We'll find something for you."

* * *

Going home was actually a relief for Terry. It had been a hard six months. They had been paddling upstream nonstop and it hadn't been hard for him to say, "Let's quit." Bert and Bill saw it as failure, but Terry and Gilbert saw it as a stepping stone.

At least now he was going to have something that would steadily move forward, rather than put him in the hole. He'd heard enough about business failures to know that the initial setbacks could stop your future. He talked to Myrna about it one night not long after he'd moved home.

"I always saw it as a stepping stone toward something else. Even though I didn't know what that something else was. Do you know what I mean?"

She had smiled and nodded. She was so happy to have him home again, especially because of the talks they had together. Terry had been quiet and reserved for the first few days, but the more they were together, the more he opened up. They talked as they always had about the little things they were thinking, the things they observed during the day.

The sound of Terry's laughter was like music filling their home--a music she had missed very much.

Sometimes their conversations became serious. One afternoon she had asked Terry to tell her about any resentments he might feel, anything that she might have done or said that hurt him.

He had to think a long time before he could remember anything. "Well, there was one time you and I were together and we saw a pretty girl. And I said, 'I'd like to ask her out.' And you said, 'Terry, you have to remember you're in a wheelchair.' "

She couldn't remember the incident but she knew he wouldn't have made it up. "I'm sorry, Terry, but if I said that, I didn't mean it. I think you can go with any girl you want to. I don't even think of you as handicapped, Terry. As far as I'm concerned, you aren't handicapped."

Myrna gave Terry a hug. "I love you, Terry," she said. "Promise me you'll always remember that."

* * *

Gilbert had accepted Terry's decision to quit his art career without argument. He'd hoped the business could be a success for the boys' sake, but he had to admire Terry's judgment in deciding to stop.

They found a house in Portland, two miles from the Highland community, next door to the home of Roy Drusky, the Grand Ole Opry star. Roy was a member of their church and had spent many nights at the hospital with Terry, when the Wilkses had needed his friendship the most.

The house was one story, with good wheelchair access and a walk-in basement apartment for Terry's attendant. It took Gilbert and the rest of the family four days to get everything unpacked and make the house liveable.

There was only one other thing Gilbert had left to do. He had to have the lawsuit resolved, one way or the other. They had done everything they could do. The insurance company could take months to decide whether to settle out of court and he was ready for a decision now. The money had become almost irrelevant to Gilbert. He had simply accepted the fact that he would have to support Terry for the rest of his life, and he had begun to plan his life accordingly. Perhaps it would mean a change in their lifestyle. So be it. He just wanted the lawsuit over with. But he believed they would win. He believed there WAS a reward for doing what was morally right.

Gilbert talked to Hal Hardin and the attorney suggested

Gilbert write a letter expressing his feelings and making a final offer to the insurance company. He would send the letter to the opposing attorneys before Christmas.

On December 19,1983 Gilbert wrote to Hardin and his partner, Bernie Durham:

Dear Hal and Bernie:

You asked us to give some thought to a proposed settlement, and to share it with you.

Honestly, we feel that the amount first asked for is not unreasonable. We understand the limitations of organizations to pay large sums such as this. We realize that God has blessed our family and given us the ability to rise above the devastating results of such an injury. Many, many families cannot cope with this type of situation and the injured person finds himself in a nursing home with his mind and body wasting away to an early death and the family going through a type of nervous breakdown.

With God's help, we intend to rise above the before mentioned; keeping our family intact; keeping Terry active and productive; and hopefully help others in the area of gymnastics from falling into the same fate because of the same contributing factors that caused Terry's injuries.

Naturally for the sake of Terry, our family, friends, and loved ones at Highland, we wish that conditions would have been different so that Terry would not have been permanently disabled and forced to bring this lawsuit. And it is our desire that through the efforts of researchers, some day, Terry, along with thousands of others, will walk again, or that through an act of God, Terry will be healed and can give full credit to his Maker. But until that time, the daily and monthly expenses to make Terry's life as near normal as possible are staggering.

In the interest of all concerned we propose a moderate settlement. This will go toward medical costs including

attendants to help make Terry independent to pursue an
occupation in which he can find satisfaction and feel that he is
contributing to society. We realize that this falls far short of
his expected lifetime expenses, but we trust that with God's
help, he will be able to improve enough to hold a job, thus
contributing his share to society.

The letter continued, but that was the point. They had come down to a more than reasonable offer considering that the projected cost of his lifetime care was over $1 million, the request for less than half of that would barely give Terry the income he needed to pay for his continued care.

* * *

It was a happy Christmas in the Wilks household that year. They missed Diane and Eddie, who were in the Marshall Islands serving as student teachers, but it was nice for Terry to have time alone with his parents and with David. The separation from his family had not been all fun and games. He missed them more than he'd realized. Now that he was home, he planned to have as good a life as he could.

He thought a lot about what he wanted to do, letting his mind wander back to all the things he'd done, before his accident and after. He went all the way back to his childhood, his earliest memories of what he wanted to be.

When he was a kid, he'd always wanted to be an architect or an engineer. He remembered the hovercraft he'd ordered from *Popular Mechanics Magazine* and tried to build. He'd always wanted to build things—mechanical things. And he still did. He could draw. That was a necessity. He was good with numbers.

Terry lay awake nights as 1983 came to an end, thinking about what his life was going to be. And the more he thought about it, the more he thought that someday he would be an engineer, just like he'd always planned.

* * *

After Christmas, Gilbert suggested that Terry accept Bert's invitation to go down to Miami for a couple of weeks before he started to work at the press. It would be good for his health, especially with another cold Tennessee winter in full swing. Besides, Bert would be starting back to school soon for the winter quarter, and this would probably be their last time together.

They'd driven down in the van and stayed at the home of some of Bert's relatives. It was warm in Florida, but Terry kept the heater on in his room anyway. He wasn't feeling well at all. He hadn't wanted to say anything, but after a week he could recognize all the signs of another urinary tract infection.

Terry was tired and dejected. He didn't know how many more times he could overcome the anger and self-pity and humiliation he felt everytime his body broke down on him.

He had Bert call his parents back in Portland to let them know he was sick. He might have to be coming back earlier than expected.

"That's good," Gilbert said. "You need to come home now anyway."

"What do you mean?" Terry asked.

"It looks like the settlement's gone through."

Terry stared straight ahead for a second. "What?"

"The insurance company's lawyers called Hal Hardin this morning. They're ready to accept our terms. It's still preliminary but he wants you close by in case we need to sign anything. So why don't you come on home."

"How much will it be?"

"It's what we requested, Terry, but we're going to have to invest it wisely, because your expenses are going to use most of it up."

Terry closed his eyes and let his head fall back.

"So why don't you come on home."

"Okay."

They hung up after a few more pleasantries and Terry sat quietly by the phone until Bert came in to see what had happened.

"I won my lawsuit, Bert," Terry said. "I won."

"Hey, I always knew you'd be rich," Bert said. "So what are you going to do now?"

"I don't know." He looked up at the ceiling as he felt the tears start coming into his eyes. "Freedom," he said to himself. "I have my freedom."

Follow
Your
Heart

SUMMER 1987

Three years have elapsed since Terry won the lawsuit. In that time, much has changed in his life. New opportunities, new friends and new challenges have presented themselves to him, and he has responded with a sense of purpose that he has developed in the difficult years since his accident.

Winning the lawsuit had an effect on Terry's life just as profound--in the opposite way--as the accident had on his old life. Where his injury had robbed him of freedom, the settlement had given it back in the form of personal opportunity.

He had been thinking about what he would do with that opportunity for a long time, and the moment the lawsuit was settled, the dreams became reality.

All the way home from Miami with Bert in the van, Terry had thought about what he would do. He had long imagined himself becoming an engineer. Was engineering something he could do, or was it meant to remain a fantasy? He would have to go back to school, probably for five or six years, if he wanted to earn a degree.

There were obstacles in his path, he knew, but engineering was what he wanted to do. By the time he arrived back in Tennessee after winning the lawsuit, Terry's mind was made up. He was ready to begin the long, demanding journey toward becoming an engineer.

Terry spent a brief time in Portland with his parents before returning to Collegedale and enrolling in the pre-engineering program at Southern College. He had felt a new excitement at being able to pay his own tuition, and an even greater excitement when he bought his first home, about a mile from campus.

Terry's house was a modern, green shingle, two story house on a dead end street called Scenic View Drive. The view from Terry's house was best out the back, where a tall stand of pine trees and several sycamores bordered the property. Picking out the furniture for the inside had been his first present to himself after the lawsuit. They'd asked Hal Hardin what they should do with the money.

"Put it away," Hardin had said. "Live on the interest. Adjusted for inflation, of course. But you owe it to yourself, after all the heartaches, to treat yourself to something special. Spend a small part on anything you want."

So he'd used the money to buy furniture.

That first year after the settlement, Terry fell in love with the idea of becoming an engineer. The detailed, technical thinking required to conceive and execute a good design was just the kind of intellectual challenge he liked most. And yet there was still the opportunity to be creative, to imagine new structural and mechanical configurations and then methodically find ways to make them work.

In his spare time, Terry began imagining a design for a new wheelchair. He had always been unhappy with the options he had to choose from, so he quietly set out to engineer a new option.

"I've always believed people should have a choice in wheelchairs, just like they have a choice in cars," he says now, reflecting on why he decided to begin building a new chair. "There were   certain things I wanted in a wheelchair, that I couldn't find. I wanted it to be very stable and secure, but I also wanted it to be comfortable and I wanted it to look good. So I decided to build a chair with those features, plus a few more."

Terry realizes that designing a new type of wheelchair is not something he will be able to accomplish quickly or easily, but his determination to work on it is indicative of his personal drive to use the abilities he has to make his own life a better one.

* * *

Conventional wisdom suggests there are five stages you go through when you sustain any injury--denial that it happened, anger, bargaining with God, depression and finally acceptance. In a way, any life-altering injury is a form of death and living through such an injury causes one to experience a similar range of emotions.

In the years since he's had financial freedom, Terry has been coming to terms with the final link in that chain-- acceptance of his fate, and his decision to build a new wheelchair was evidence of that.

Another sign of Terry's acceptance was a new understanding of his relationship with God. Terry thanked God for the freedom he'd received as a result of the settlement. He had been given an opportunity to have his own life, by the power that bestows life. He thought about people who made the decisions of their lives based on what other people thought. He could see that he had been like that when he was younger. It was the same thing as being a robot. God gave people the ability to develop themselves for a reason. He expected them to use that ability. That's what he must do,

Terry realized. He must develop the abilities God had given him--make himself useful with the abilities that still remained. He began to believe that the only difference between people was the different limits of their potential.

Terry gradually underwent a type of conversion in the years following his accident, that was accelerated after the settlement was won. He had come to find God, not out in heaven, but a heavenly God within himself.

There had been times when he wanted to scream at God. He would never forget the days and nights of pain he had spent following the accident. "God, don't you care!" he had wanted to cry. There had been five or six times when he had felt death close at hand, and only by turning inside himself, to a source of strength and power there, had he been able to defeat it. That source of strength and power was God.

Terry had never blamed God for the accident. God hadn't made it happen. God had simply allowed it to happen.

God's gift to man was life, Terry believed. MAN'S GIFT TO GOD WAS LIVING. That was why Terry wanted to have his own life. He wanted to live up to his God-given potential.

As Terry began to see his life in a new perspective, he began to see that there were many strong characteristics about his life before the accident that had become even stronger since.

"I always felt I had to go somewhere. I had to do something. And I think that helped me after the accident, because then I felt like I was being pinned down and I could either let myself be pinned, or I could throw it over. I had one choice or the other, to quit or give it all I had."

Terry's challenge was to channel his energy in a constuctive way, and the more he did that, the more he came to find a new self-acceptance that made him feel better, not only about himself, but about other people.

He no longer wondered if people befriended him out of sympathy or pity. He knew that no matter what attracted people to him at first, given time they would either stay or go away because of how they felt about him, not about his condition.

His changing attitude toward girls was a reflection of his new self-acceptance. Realtionships with girls had been one of the hardest things Terry had had to deal with since the accident. He had experienced emotional pain many times, and with each experience he had learned a new lesson about life.

"For a long time, rejection by a girl really hurt me deeply, because I felt like it meant they couldn't see past the wheelchair...they couldn't see me," Terry remembers. "The lesson I'm learning is that my happiness depends on how I feel about myself, not how someone else feels about me. I don't feel like I have to have a girlfriend anymore. I still like girls, I like them a lot, but I like girls who are friends first.

"I say I'm still learning because I'm not 100 percent positive about girls or anything else. I still get depressed sometimes and feel sorry for myself. But I don't let myself dwell on thoughts of my physical condition, because if I did, I wouldn't try any of the things I'm trying. I don't believe in saying 'I can't,' because to say that is to die."

Dr. Cushman described Terry's way of dealing with his reality as "selective denial."

"We all do it," Dr. Cushman said, "but we don't all use it in such a positive way as Terry does. That is a mark of maturity. Terry is wise beyond his years."

Another of his doctors, Samuel Stover, said, "A person's personality before the injury is a more important measure of how successfully they'll deal with physical disablility. It doesn't help everyone to mature. The will to want to make something of your life must be there before the accident."

* * *

In the Spring of 1984, while Terry was finding his new enthusiasm for engineering in Chattanooga, Diane was living half way around the world in the Marshall Islands, teaching math, science, English, spelling and Bible to a class of second grade island children. Diane had started attending Southern College a year before and was in the South Pacific as part of a student teacher program. Also teaching school there, on an island 250 miles away, was Eddie Nolan.

Diane and Eddie had grown very close in the years since they'd met. Diane felt a closeness to Eddie and an ability to communicate with him that she had never felt with anyone before.

That summer, Gilbert, Myrna and David flew to the Marshall Islands to meet Diane and Eddie. Together they planned to continue on to Asia, Europe and home to America, where they would record their adventures in a series of articles called "Happiness Around the World" for the Happiness television booklet.

It was obvious to Gilbert and Myrna on the trip that their daughter felt something special for Eddie. And then in Venice, on a romantic stroll after sunset, Eddie asked for Diane's hand in marriage.

Diane and Eddie were married on June 29, 1985, in a quiet and dignified ceremony in Portland.

Following their wedding, Eddie and Diane moved to Collegedale, where Eddie was finishing his senior year at Southern College. They lived half a mile from Terry's house, and their new proximity provided an opportunity for Diane and Terry to spend time together and find the closeness they had known all of their lives--until the accident.

Diane had felt a distance from her brother since the accident. He wasn't the same Terry. He was in a wheelchair. She didn't know what to say to him, how to communicate the love and sorrow she felt. In fact, she wasn't sure if she really knew how she felt, but the more time they spent together, the more she was able to express the grief she had kept bottled up for so long.

Terry's closeness to his parents also was growing stronger. He could see more and more the special confidence that his mother had in him. Myrna's belief in Terry's ability to overcome adversity had never waivered. Terry was capable of having anything he set his mind to. She had watched that trait blossom in him, despite all of the obstacles, from the day he was born. He was still the same Terry.

With Gilbert, however, there was more of a strain. He had watched Terry's progress with growing admiration and respect, yet Gilbert could not stop worrying about his son. Terry was still young and impatient with life. He wanted to do too much, too fast. But when Gilbert said slow down, Terry reacted as if Gilbert were trying to run his life. Still, as a father, he could not relax that drive inside him to look after his son.

For Terry, the closeness with his family seemed to conflict with his new-found independence. He relished the idea of making his own decisions. Buying a house had been an exhilirating experience. Living on his own with paid attendants to care for him gave him an even greater sense of freedom.

Then in late 1985, Terry came to another decision--to move to Florida. The move made sense to Terry for a lot of reasons. First and foremost was the warmth. Summers were warm in Tennessee, but the winters could be bitter, and when they were, he felt it in his bones. Florida did not have the mountainous landscape of Collegedale which made wheelchair mobility so difficult, and its laws were much more attuned to the needs of the handicapped. For those and other reasons, Terry decided to move.

Gilbert and Myrna were apprehensive about Terry moving so far away. They had felt hope as their relationship began to grow closer, but now that Terry wanted to move 750 miles away, they feared that a new emotional distance would be created as well. And for the first few months after he moved to Winter Park, Terry did seem to be pulling away from them.

He was making new friends, becoming involved in new activities and enjoying himself. But Terry needed his family, and as he began to realize that, he also realized that it was possible to have his independence and his freedom, and still be close to his family.

When he talked about his feelings with his parents, their hearts went out to him. They wanted that closeness again, more than anything in their lives. So in the Summer of 1987, the Wilks family moved to Longwood, Florida, to be near Terry.

The decision to leave Tennessee had not been easy. There were a lot of memories for Gilbert and Myrna. When they drove the streets of their hometown they observed certain landmarks with a new sense of emotion. There was pain, mixed with satsifaction everywhere. The gymnasium particularly evoked special feelings for them. For so long, when they looked at the gym, their thoughts went back to he terrible evening of Terry's accident. But more and more, when they saw the gym, they were reminded of the morning of his graduation and the tremendous sense of victory they'd felt as the entire congregation rose in applause.

So many times they had feared that the problems were insurmountable. Yet they had faith, and now they could see that their faith had been rewarded. And the only reason they could tell themselves that was because of Terry. The victory was in Terry's attitude.

* * *

The sun is shining and Terry is sitting outside, feeling good. His family is now close by and his dream of becoming an engineer seems closer to reality than ever. He is enrolled at Valencia College and is taking two courses, which gives him time to continue work on his wheelchair design. It is a complicated process, but one he still finds exciting.

Eddie and Diane live nearby and have already started a business of their own, with Gilbert's help. They have opened a video rental store called Happiness Video, which specializes in wholesome family entertainment videos, and in the first few months, they already have demonstrated that there is a good market for their type of store.

Terry is very happy that Diane and he are close again, and he and Eddie have developed a running chess match.

Gilbert and Myrna are still getting settled at their new home nearby. David is now eight years old and seems to be happier about the move than anybody, unless of course it's Grandma Wilks.

Having his family nearby has given Terry a sense of security that he hasn't experienced since before the accident, and it feels good.

Since moving to Florida, Terry has stayed in regular contact with Dr. Barth Green in Miami. He has watched with excitement and fascination as Dr. Green's dream of a major initiative to defeat paralysis has suddenly taken shape.

"The Miami Project" as it is called, has declared its goal to end paralysis in five years, and with the help of Nick Buoniconti, whose son Marc was paralyzed as the result of a football injury, the Miami Project has the support and the research capabilities to possibly achieve that goal.

As Louise McKnew told Terry: "Thirty years ago, 20,000 people a year were contracting polio, the same number who today suffer paralysis as a result of injury. Today, polio is a rare problem. Who's to say that 30 years from now paralysis won't be considered rare as well."

For Terry, the Miami Project is a reminder of the constant emotional battle he fought and continues to fight--hoping on the one hand that a cure for paralysis can be found, while reminding himself everyday to accept his paralysis and make the most of his life here and now.

"I have to believe both ways," Terry says. "I have to have hope that the miracle can happen, but I also have to believe that it may not happen for me. Otherwise I start slipping into that fantasy of what my life will be like when I walk again. I can't do that. The best advice I ever received about miracles is that they come when you don't expect them, so don't expect them."

Terry's acceptance of his paralysis, and his hope, have come despite a great deal of pain, mental despair and adversity that could have caused him to lose hope. He has accepted his limitations and learned to live with them. Indeed, he has come to understand the difference between limitations and handicaps.

"I don't believe in physical handicaps," Terry says. "Physical disability has nothing to do with the human being inside the body, the Self. If a person has a birthmark on their face, or a clubfoot, they are not handicapped unless they see themselves that way. The only handicaps are the ones in our minds."

Terry Wilks is a whole human being. Losing the movement of his body did not change that. And he has discovered the wholeness of his being by turning inward and listening to his instincts. There he has found the acceptance of God, the acceptance of his family and friends, and the acceptance of himself.

He has found happiness. He has followed his heart.